Taxation Without Representation
Fourth Edition

Can the U.S. Avoid Another "Boston Tea Party?"

This book relies on the Constitution, the founding documents, Articles of Association, Declaration of Rights and Grievances, Declaration of Independence, and the Bill of Rights.

Taxation without Representation unearths and explores a massive dilemma for U.S. Citizens. The US began without representation. Then, the Colonies fought a war of independence to acquire representation. Now, our beloved representatives have fallen for the candy-coated wiles of the new kids on the block--obscenely rich mega-corporations and members of the establishment of both parties.

This book offers a walk-though about how our government once was, how it improved, and how it again eroded and regressed from freedom to a new set of oppressive roots. The book highlights the major issues affecting the American worker, particularly the wholesale exportation of jobs to legal and illegal foreign nationals. The book also discusses how both political parties are preventing independent candidates from appearing on ballots and the problems presented by voting machines surreptitiously designed with technology that enables an interested party's surrogates to manipulate and even override the people's choices.

Our representative democratic republic is definitely in trouble. We have the biggest bumbling set of idiots ever supposedly representing us, while scobbing up every perquisite possible for themselves. While pointing out definitively that we pay too much in taxes, this book also offers a number of unique solutions to help get us back on a track of which the founders would smile. You will too. Enjoy!

BRIAN W. KELLY

Copyright © 2010, 2014, 2016, 2018 Brian W. Kelly
Author Brian W. Kelly
Taxation without Representation Fourth Edition
Can the U.S. Avoid Another "Boston Tea Party"?

All rights reserved: No part of this book may be reproduced or transmitted in any form, or by any means, electronic or mechanical, including photocopying, recording, scanning, faxing, or by any information storage and retrieval system, without permission from the publisher, LETS GO PUBLISH, in writing.

Disclaimer: Though judicious care was taken throughout the writing and the publication of this work that the information contained herein is accurate, there is no expressed or implied warranty that all information in this book is 100% correct. Therefore, neither LETS GO PUBLISH, nor the author accepts liability for any use of this work.

Trademarks: A number of products and names referenced in this book are trade names and trademarks of their respective companies.

Referenced Material: The information in this book has been obtained through personal and third-party observations, interviews, and copious research. Where unique information has been provided or extracted from other sources, those sources are acknowledged within the text of the book itself or at the end of the chapter in the Sources Section. Thus, there are no formal footnotes nor is there a bibliography section. Any picture that does not have a source was taken from various sites on the Internet with no credit attached. If resource owners would like credit in the next printing, please email publisher.

Published by: LETS GO PUBLISH!
Publisher: Brian P. Kelly **Publisher:** Brian P. Kelly
P.O Box 621
Wilkes-Barre, PA 18703
brian@brianpkelly.com
www.letsgopublish.com

Library of Congress Copyright Information Pending
Book Cover Design by Michele Thomas, Editing by Brian P. Kelly

ISBN Information: The International Standard Book Number (ISBN) is a unique machine-readable identification number, which marks any book unmistakably. The ISBN is the clear standard in the book industry. 159 countries and territories are officially ISBN members. The Official ISBN For this book is on the outside cover:
978-1-947402-27-0

The price for this work is :								$12.95 USD	
10	9	8	7	6	5	4	3	2	1
Release Date:								January, 2018	

LETS GO
PUBLISH!

Dedication

I dedicate this book to Angel Kathleen and Joseph McKeown, wonderful people, wonderful first cousins and avid supporters of all of my writing efforts.

Thank You and the Best!

Acknowledgments

I appreciate all the help that I received in putting this book together, along with the 144 other books from the past.

My printed acknowledgments were once so large that book readers needed to navigate too many pages to get to page one of the text. To permit me more flexibility, I put my acknowledgment list online at www.letsgopublish.com. The list of acknowledgments continues to grow. Believe it or not, it once cost about a dollar more to print each book.

Thank you all on the big list in the sky and God bless you all for your help.

Please check out www.letsgopublish.com to read the latest version of my heartfelt acknowledgments updated for this book. Thank you all!

In this book, I received some extra special help from Dennis Grimes, Gerry Rodski, Wily Ky Eyely and her secret friends, Angel Irene McKeown Kelly, Angel Edward Joseph Kelly Sr., Angel Edward Joseph Kelly Jr., Ann Flannery, Angel James Flannery Sr., Mary Daniels, Bill Daniels, Robert Gary Daniels, Angel Sarah Janice Daniels, Angel Punkie Daniels, Joe Kelly, Diane Kelly, Angels Fluff & Puff Kelly, Brian P. Kelly, Mike P. Kelly, Katie P. Kelly; the late Benjamin Arthur Kelly, and Budmund Arthur Kelly.

Table of Contents

Acknowledgments 7

Table of Contents 9

Chapter 1 America Gained and Lost Its Independence 1

Chapter 2 We Elect Talking Heads & Empty Suits 9

Chapter 3 We Get the Government We Deserve 15

Chapter 4 Life for Politicians Will Never Be the Same ... 31

Chapter 5 The Tax "Cuts" of 2017 35

Chapter 6 Too Many Honorables 41

Chapter 7 Scientific Method 4 "Honorables" Problem ... 45

Chapter 8 A Civics Lesson: Constitutional Democracy . 69

Chapter 9: Taxes, Taxes, and More Taxes 81

Chapter 10 Civics Lesson: Lots of Taxes, Explanations. 93

Chapter 11 US: Overtaxed & Under Represented 103

Chapter 12 The Rise of Corporate Power 115

Chapter 13 The Robber Barons Are Back 129

Chapter 14 Unions Meet the Robber Baron Challenge. 143

Chapter 15 Worker Visas Take Many American Jobs.. 153

Chapter 17 Throw the Bums Out Now! 163

Chapter 18 General Solutions- 4 Future of the USA 169

Preface:

Brian W. Kelly wrote this book because our representatives in the House, the Senate, in state legislatures and city councils have forgotten their duties as representatives of the people. Additionally, the president, the governors, the mayors, and other prefects of the people in the executive branches of governments across the land have conveniently forgotten that the primary fundamentals of our representative constitutional democracy (republic) start with representation.

In the prior edition, Kelly included four poignant essays of Thomas Dawson, a great writer to help in somebody else's words put the relationship of illegal and legal immigration, greedy politicians, the unions, and corporation in proper context. This book has been enhanced so that these essays are no longer required to get the essence of this book. However, Brian did release these essays in their own stand-alone book titled, Great Political Essays from Thomas Dawson. These are very good and very inexpensive available on Amazon and Kindle.

"No taxation without representation" was the catch phrase in the period of 1763-1776 to summarize the major grievance of the American colonists in the Thirteen American Colonies, incipient kernels of what would later become the United States of America. When King George III of England and the English Parliament began to impose new taxes on the colonists (Stamp Act, Intolerable Acts, etc.) without their concurrence, Reverend Jonathan Mayhew of Boston coined this term during one of his sermons in Boston.

Another Bostonian, a politician by *the speak of the day*, James Otis, changed this just a bit and he is well known for the phrase, "taxation without representation is tyranny." Tyranny it was and in this book, you will see that tyranny it surely is again.

In 1773, American Colonists violently opposed the tax on tea imports at the most celebrated Tea Party of all time. The Boston Tea Party is recognized as the first experience in which the colonists acted against the Crown. Of course, the British could not accept this "illegal act" as they saw that it would undermine the authority of the Crown and Parliament. When the British Government began to crack down on these "illegal activities" performed by the colonists, the colonists chose to defend themselves in case the British Government did not hear their pleas to correct the abuses.

Though today the tea still may be contained safely in the ships in Boston Harbor, millions have expressed discontent of the government just several years ago by holding their own tea parties all over the US in protests against the American government. Bernie Sanders and Donald Trump have awakened the same spirit of "NO" today to a government that thinks it owns the people of this great country. Donald Trump is now President of our great country.

Beware the lulling idea that your government cannot be taken over by rich members of a *ruling class,* or de-facto by corporations, or even by a powerful president with disdain for capitalism. Look how close former President Obama came to destroying America. The quickest way to assure this can happen in our time is to stop paying attention; stop caring; and stop voting and to let them simply have their way.

Brian W. Kelly wrote this book because he cares, and I am publishing this book because I care. Together, BWK and I hope to energize Americans again in the still new millennium as in the 1700's. Our mantra is that this magnificent democracy, of which much blood was shed, continues to be worth fighting for.

I hope you enjoy reading this book and that you will remain vigilant and take the actions necessary so that this experiment in democracy, this United States of America can persevere and succeed for many hundreds and hundreds of more years. For now, I wish you the best! Yes, we suffer from Taxation without Representation but as we awaken to that reality, we can make it much better by paying attention to who we make our elected representatives.

Sincerely

Brian P. Kelly, Editor & Publisher

About the Author

Brian Kelly retired as an Assistant Professor in the Business Information Technology (BIT) Program at Marywood University, where he also served as the IBM i and Midrange Systems Technical Advisor to the IT Faculty. Kelly designed, developed, and taught many college and professional courses. He continues as a contributing technical editor to a number of technical industry magazines, including "The Four Hundred" and "Four Hundred Guru," published by IT Jungle. Kelly often has written for blogs such as Conservative Action Alerts.

Kelly is a former IBM Senior Systems Engineer. His specialty was problem solving for customers as well as implementing advanced operating systems and software on his client's machines. Brian is the author of 144 books and hundreds of magazine articles. Over half of his books and articles are about patriotic topics. Brian has been a frequent speaker at conferences throughout the United States.

Kelly was a candidate for the US Congress from Pennsylvania in 2010 and he ran for Mayor in his home town in 2015. He loves America but has no love for corrupt officials.

Chapter 1 America Gained and Lost Its Independence

Our celebration is shallow today

We celebrate Independence Day every July 4, as we memorialize a day from July 4, 1776, in Philadelphia, Pennsylvania, when the Continental Congress formally adopted the Declaration of Independence. The Declaration of Independence was written by Thomas Jefferson to announce to the world that the United States of America was declaring its independence from King George III and Great Britain.

Some suggest this was very much a Brexit of our own. The Revolutionary War was well underway by July 4, 1776, as 442 days earlier, the shot heard round the world and other shots were fired at Lexington, Massachusetts. The Lexington battle is considered to be the beginning of the first battle of the American Revolutionary War.

It certainly was not the end of the Revolutionary War. On the Contrary, the Revolution was underway, and the purpose of this undertaking was to wake up the British that America was very upset. It was a major notification to the British and the rest of mankind that the US had had enough of British Imperialism.

The United States formally announced that it no longer wished to accept British rule. This was a big deal and a lot of people lost their lives making true independence happen in America. The British had become the dominant country in the colonies by the time of the revolt. If they had been fair to the colonists, there never would have been a war.

Britain was #1 in America since the early 17th century when the Virginia Company became the Virginia Colony in 1624, the first of the original thirteen British colonies.

Britain was big on colonization at the time. The American Colonies were not the only part of the world - or even the only part of the Americas that were subject to British rule. England was the most powerful country on earth and they exerted control over much of Canada, the Caribbean, and South America. When the British got greedy, Americans were not about to take it anymore.

The British became bullies

The British excuse for its behavior was that ruling and protecting the world, including the American Colonies was very expensive. Guarding colonies and invading new lands for imperialistic reasons took a lot of money and Britain was often at war. They had gotten pretty good at war with all their experience. For the American Colonies to take on the British would not be an easy task.

As happened in America, throughout the world of British fiefdoms, not all countries were in agreement about who owned what land and who had what rights, and so fighting wars, big or small, was often the only apparent remedy. This is what happened in the mid-18th century when Great Britain found itself battling a number of different tough countries - but primarily France - in the Seven Years' War. When that war ended in 1763, Great Britain clearly won but the long period of fighting had come at a significant financial cost. The British government was nearly bankrupt.

The King was theoretically an absolute ruler at the time, though Parliament had its say. The King became fixated on raising revenue. The richness of the American lands seemed like a great place to grab some cash. The big problem for England, however, was that unless the American Colonies of Britain agreed to tax themselves, just as districts in England, imposing taxes would be illegal. But then again, the King could theoretically break any law he wished.

There was no apparently better way to raise revenue for the Crown than a series of taxes and tariffs? Who could possibly be better targets for such revenue measures than subjects who lived far away - like the American colonists. The British expected the distance to muffle the complaining? There was just one problem with this plan: The King underestimated exactly how irritated the colonists would become.

Their complaints were well heard all the way across the Atlantic to England.

The Intolerable Acts

In early history classes taught in the third grade, American students were introduced to the causes of the Revolutionary War. The new and unauthorized taxes were a major source of angst for the colonists. The first big tax imposed was the Stamp Act of 1765.

Unlike postage stamps, taxation stamps were an official confirmation of compliance with a certain rule or requirement. In this case, materials which were printed and used in the colonies, like magazines and newspapers, were required to be produced on special stamped paper and embossed with a revenue stamp, confirming that tax had been paid to Mother England.

Colonists, of course, didn't like it, and the Stamp Act was quickly repealed the next year.

The second attempt at raising revenue for the Crown, was actually a series of acts known as the Townshend Acts of 1767 (individually, they were the Revenue Act of 1767, the Indemnity Act, the Commissioners of Customs Act, the Vice Admiralty Court Act, and the New York Restraining Act).

These taxes were a little bit different than the Stamp Act - they were indirect taxes. However, the result was no different. The colonists weren't happy, and the Townshend Acts were partially repealed. The Crown was determined to get its due from Americans.

In 1773, King and Parliament imposed the Tea Act on top of the remaining Townshend Acts. Another tax on the colonists was the last straw for many Americans, even though it wasn't a completely new tax. What the Tea Act did was keep in place the duty (tax) on tea imported to the colonies (already in place under the Townshend Act).

The purpose of the Tea Act was not to raise revenue per se, but to give the East India Tea Company a trade advantage, cutting out the ability of the colonists to do business on own their terms. Tax or not, the colonists viewed the Tea Act as another stifling way in which they were unjustly being controlled.

The colonists would not stand down. They figured that the best way to stand up to the Tea Act was to turn away the ships that were carrying tea headed for the colonies. They were successful in Philadelphia and in New York - but not in Boston. The Governor of Massachusetts would not permit the ships to be turned back even though the colonists would not allow the ships to be unloaded in the harbor. It was a stand-off. To end it, the colonists masqueraded as Indians and snuck onto the ships and dumped out the tea. This celebrated event in history is the Boston Tea Party.

The Tea Party that occurred on December 16, 1773, did not immediately lead to the Declaration of Independence or the Revolutionary War, but war was definitely brewing with all that tea in the harbor. It was well before the shots at Lexington and before the Declaration of Independence. The Boston Tea Party, nonetheless made the British Parliament irate and ready to "get even."

Parliament felt that England was so powerful, they could exert their will on the colonists to get back at them for their "little party." They attempted to punish the Americans through a series of laws called the Coercive Acts. Under these nasty acts, among other things, Boston Harbor was closed to merchant shipping; town meetings were banned, and the British commander of North American forces was appointed to be the governor of Massachusetts.

The colonists had enough. They were not going to take it anymore and the actions they took in response would in fact create a war with Great Britain.

To gain a solid voice in their dissent, they convened the First Continental Congress in Philadelphia on September 5, 1774. At this meeting, they considered their next steps. Resistance against the British increased and before too long, those first shots in Massachusetts were fired triggering the Revolutionary War. Finally, over a year later, the Second Continental Congress convened in Philadelphia.

On July 2, 1776, the Second Continental Congress voted to separate from Great Britain. Two days later, on July 4, the Declaration of Independence, written mostly by Thomas Jefferson, was formally adopted by 12 of the 13 colonies. The one holdout at the time, the state of New York, approved it a couple of weeks later.

The Declaration of Independence is written as a letter to the King of England. When the Declaration was being drafted, the colonists felt that it was important that the exact reasons for their unhappiness were made clear. The largest section of the Declaration - after the lines that we all memorized in grade school - is that list of grievances. Of course, taxes were a major set of items included in the grievances

The history of the present King of Great Britain is a history of repeated injuries and usurpations, all having in direct object the establishment of an absolute Tyranny over these States. To prove this, let Facts be submitted to a candid world.
...

For imposing Taxes on us without our Consent:

The word "Consent" was important. Under the British Constitution, no British subjects could be taxed without the consent of their representatives in Parliament. But the colonies didn't elect representatives to Parliament. They were, however, clearly being taxed. The colonists considered the constant imposition of taxes without a vote to be unconstitutional. It was, they felt, "taxation without representation."

The idea that the colonists had such little control over their own lives didn't just lead to the drafting of the Declaration of Independence and the accompanying vote, it set the United States down the road to real independence. In 1783, with the signing of the Treaty of Paris, the United States formally became an independent nation.

But the date that we most associate with our independence is the day that those in the Continental Congress were brave enough to officially declare it to the world: July 4. And, so we celebrate our independence every July 4, as we are now a country that has taxation with full representation. Or are we?

Representative Democracy

If we truly were a representative democracy today, then our representatives would exercise our will when they met to make the laws of the nation. Many Americans believe that the problem today with our representative democracy is our representatives have begun to represent themselves rather than the people.

In the formation of the country after America gained its independence and we became a constitutional republic, the founders refused to permit political parties. The wisdom of this decision is evident even today as we see that many of the root problems in the political system in America is because of what many see as the "two-party system."

A growing number of Americans today choose not to identify with one of our two major political parties. Record numbers of Americans call themselves "independent." Nonetheless most still favor one party over the other.

A typical reaction for those who vote given conflicting views on social welfare and abortion: "When it comes to voting, I have to hold my nose! I don't enjoy it, and I usually don't feel very good about the ballot I've cast."

The two-party system does not do Americans justice. Originally, Congressional representatives were apportioned at about 33,000 people for one representative. Today with major population growth, it is about 700,000 to 1 representative. No wonder Congressmen act like they are lords. With technology, and a bigger Capitol building with state caucuses determining who could speak on behalf of a state, the numbers of representatives could be brought back to about 30,000 but chances are that won't ever happen until we the people revolt again.

The real resistance to such congressional reform would come from the self-centered body of Congress itself. The Democratic and Republican parties are also the problem, not the solution. They enjoy a duopoly and that too is unfair.

No third party, or even a faction within the parties, can disrupt their stranglehold, especially when redistricting and gerrymandering have created solidly Democratic and Republican seats. Only a man with billions of dollars such as Donald Trump could take on the SWAMP and win. Thank God but few individuals have Trump's resources.

Americans must begin to demand such reforms and/or more regularly send entrenched self-serving representatives packing for home.

So, what we have is a system in which members and even candidates continue to reflect the more partisan positions of the party, regardless of the will of the people. Although roughly 40% of Americans describe themselves as independent, Washington continues to be driven by the right- and left-wing believers who form the base of each of the parties, resulting in acrimony and stalemate.

Until we come to grips with this as a nation and we begin to hold our representatives accountable by firing them more often, we will have to bear the stain and corrupt stench they have created in the hallowed halls of our federal government.

If you think it cannot be changed, you're right.

But, if you think it can be changed, it can only be changed with the participation of all Americans of good will. Do not trust the government.

Chapter 2 We Elect Talking Heads & Empty Suits

America Is a Representative Democracy?

When the following thought marched into my mind only a few short years ago, "America is a representative democracy," I began to ask myself, isn't it time that we actually had some real "representation" from our so-called representative government? The way it now works provides far too much separation between us, the electors, and them, the elected officials coordinating our pooled resources for the alleged benefit of "everyone." But who is everyone? A genuinely compelling concern for our government or a Disney-like utopian myth?

I propose the latter. Our government is wholly unaccountable. Our lawmakers have no trouble going with the flow and committing us to years of debt without even taking the time to read the legislation for which they vote. Even worse, its members, allegedly our civil servants, do not even seem to care for our own wellbeing. They care for their leadership and themselves, but they just can't get it into their heads that we the people count at all.

While running for office, it seems that incumbent and aspiring prospective officials saturate our consciousness day-in and day-out, wheedling us into their self-perpetuating power games with promises of responsiveness, unity, and even candor. Yet, even then, only one primary concern lurks on their minds, that *sine qua non* of their very daily existence, the next election.

A forthcoming election could be as distant as two years and still your impending loss of job, perhaps due to a plant relocating to China, or one closing in Michigan, is at best a secondary afterthought to the very men and women promising you change, when you want it, and stability, again when they believe you want it.

Unfortunately, their priorities are one dimensional and your job going to China or just no longer existing, isn't the focus. Eventually they get re-elected by us, and go off to Washington for yet another term. The cycle starts again with the eternal candidate alternating between Washington and their well-insulated, gated communities far enough from the common people that they don't have to care what you think.

It's Never Them

When they are about to raise your taxes, they are particularly inconspicuous. Being numbed to the excesses and decadent corruption of everyday politics, you may not expect communication and straight answers and, so you are not disappointed. You hear about the tax issues on TV or in the paper, not from your elected because your opinion on the matter really doesn't matter. They would rather converse via cellular or Blackberry or iPhones with some of the only entities who truly can garner their attention—co-Congressmen, the affluent, the corrupt media, and of course, major campaign donors.

Discussing an important issue with you, while seeming like a charming noble way for a representative to spend an afternoon, is discarded as wanton. It's dismissed simply because it would not tangibly benefit anyone's reelection campaign which, as we have all learned, begins the day oaths of office are sworn.

They want us to think that any tax increase is caused by imaginary rival agents or economic forces beyond their control. They will convey this to us with the sole purpose of acquiring our hard-earned money. Apparently, they promise, any burdens will fall on some imaginary "other person" and we will remain unscathed.

Horrifically but as expected though, when we get our tax bills from the bureaucracy, we find out that we were that "other" person. Since the bureaucracy sent us the bill, we blame the bureaucracy, and again we let our politicians off the hook, just like our "representative" hoped we would. And again, they live to run for another election, their only professional motivation in life.

Talk to the Hand

Most individuals feel that their needs and opinions are not taken very seriously by elected representatives who occupy the hallowed chambers of our government buildings. We would call it a communication break-down but there really is no communication.

Despite our inability to get legislators to know our side of important issues, such as taxation, jobs, illegal aliens, etc., and more recently, bailouts, and healthcare, we treat them with too much respect. We intrinsically know that they care only about the desires and opinions of pressure groups, lobbyists, corporate executives and owners, as well as the plain old rich.

Only these voices reach our representatives. Yet, time and time again, we let them off the hook. Politicians cut themselves off from their electorate by choice to be spared from accountability. Yet, whenever necessary, they make a resurfacing experience and always in time for the next election. Why are we so nice to them?

You may not see them in action when they work the halls of congress but you do see them work the wedding halls when it is the height of the election season. In Congress, the typical representative appears to have some sort of godly mandate, on the basis of which, whatever they put forward must be good for everybody. However, whether it is a good idea or not, and they rarely are, you know the idea more than likely came from the whispers of the chosen elite. Politicians do not serve most of their electorate and they get away with it because again, we do not hold them accountable, and we do not break their pattern by showing up on their doorsteps with our needs.

It's time to fire them—every one of them!

What would happen to the placid world of the politician if its constituency took them to task? What might happen to these politicos if the citizens suddenly became extremely active? How would the elected representative handle such a massive increase in constituent contact? Would they become beneficent and magnanimous? Or would they choose the hermitage approach and lock the gates and doors and hope the rabble will go away?

Especially if we think they would never put up with our entreaties, we should deluge them anyway and help power our representative democracy back to working order. In our hearts, we know we would see nothing more than congressional aides coming out of the woodwork to "see if they can help matters." That of course is code for "see if they can shut us up!" And, for their lack of efforts on our behalf, we should do the only humane thing: fire them! Throw the bums out. They've had their day.

Regular people are taking Notice

There is a clear and fundamental problem with our government, even when we are on different sides of most of the other issues. In Mitt Romney's campaign, he said that Washington was "broken." With Obama right before Trump, it may be just "broke."

Either way, it is almost beyond repair. For the broken government that gave us the infamous Bush Dubai Ports deal, whose ex-Presidents represent foreign nations, and who have passed laws such as the "uniform labeling of products" fiasco, a fellow citizen of mine, Rik Reppe, a regular guy and self-described performer, writer, raconteur, and occasional business geek, ripped the establishment a new item in his blog at the URL below.

http://reppe.blogs.com/reppecom/2006/03/because_we_get_.html

Reppe believes that we the people get exactly what we deserve because we elect these talking heads and empty suits, who owe their allegiance to some corporation someplace. To demonstrate the rage that is out there in cyberspace about what an absolutely abysmal bunch of political louts run our government, I picked two paragraphs from Rik's rants on the labeling topic. Though many things have been Obama's fault for eight long years, even more as days go by, lack of representation is not a recent phenomenon. These caught Rik's ire, for example, back, pre-Obama, in March, 2006

"But why should we believe the House of Representatives is looking out for us and not sucking at the corporate t...t? That's easy. You know the House has got your back...you know they're grandstanding for votes...on any and all issues on which no public hearings are held. Because we all know that politicians who are looking out for the people hate it when those efforts are brought to the attention of the people. Hate it, hate it, hate it. The last thing...the very last thing in the whole wide political universe any politician wants to do in an election year is to trumpet efforts to help the voters thus securing easy camera and soundbite time.

...

And ain't it grand that on the same day the Senate passed a completely impotent and toothless "lobbying reform" bill that contains no actual provision to enforce the increased disclosure the impotent and toothless product of their collective minds created (passed by a vote of 90-8 proving that as much as I want this to be a Republican issue it f...ing well isn't) it takes up an issue that had been voted down by every Congress since 1994 and is only back to the influence of lobbyists? You may hate what our Senators are doing but you gotta love that kind of brazen chutzpa, don't you?"

Chapter 3 We Get the Government We Deserve

Do they work for somebody else?

The chasm between electors and the elected is widening as we speak. The John Does and the Jane Q. Publics have lost faith in their representatives. Many have become fully disinterested in the political process, though the healthcare "debate" and the fresh air at the "Town Meetings" may be just the cure for this malaise.

For some time, with good reason, the public has felt disenfranchised from the basic right of a citizen to participate in their democracy. Some may handle this by ignoring politics. Others may find alternative ways to attempt to influence the course of events, sometimes through friends and associates, but not always with very positive results.

Sometimes as we have seen in our history, the frustration of humans in our democracy leads to violence as in the civil rights movements and the anti-war rallies of the 1960's and the riots in Los Angeles in the 1990's. Are we there again? Perhaps the main reason that the system even seems to work is that constituents do not make many demands -- at least till now, and like Reppe says,

> "We Get The Government We Deserve."

This is the root cause that permits politicians, masquerading as our representatives, to represent others' interests. It is an understatement to suggest that representatives are out of touch with the will of the people. Even the newly elected begin to share the wealth of their constituency with others as they begin their "service." They have this need to redistribute income and now they are redistributing healthcare.

This is a common malady of the often elected and the newly elected are quickly infected. For a politician, it's "catchier" than the Swine Flu. Elected "representatives" have no problem taking your money and buying votes with it -- even if there is nothing left in the treasury.

Until they got caught by John Q., how many of the "honorables" voted originally to have the non-working and the illegal aliens receive the tax rebate of 2008? This trick was like buying future votes, but the motivation was the same. It wasn't really intended for the downtrodden, hapless, illegal foreign national struggling to make ends meet. Not a chance. It was to puff up the elected to demonstrate their magnanimity and vote-worthiness. The Congress still is getting away with this caper.

Besides your money, they will also take your means of earning a living if it serves their purposes. To please their corporate sponsors, they have no problem taking your job and giving it to a foreign national, either here in the U.S. or in the worker's home country, in China or India. They have just one mission and it is accomplished if they get elected again. The next term of office, not the current one, is all that matters. We get the government we deserve.

The House of Lords

Senators are above it all. They breathe the rarified air reserved for the Gods. If you see a Senator once in your life, it is a memorable event. Perhaps you are among the lucky. Perhaps not! Senators have so many people to represent that they operate as Lords, clearly of the nobility (though nobility is expressly forbidden by the Constitution), and they have no need to ever mingle with the common folk. They can't anyway.

In Pennsylvania, for example, the state in which I live, it is the 6th most populated state in the U.S. with an estimated population of 12,500,000. That means that between the two senators, each gets to work with over six million people. No way no how! The Senators know they do not have to represent the people and, so they represent whoever they choose and they still get sent back every six years like it is an entitlement. A sure thing. We get the government we deserve.

The House of Commons

What about our representatives? Why don't we ever see them? Remember that our Constitution clearly specifies the number of senators and representatives. The ratio is fixed at 1 representative for each 30,000 in the electorate. Now, that is still a high ratio but it is workable.

Regardless of what is in the Constitution, however, in the year 1911, the representatives themselves decided to break this basic tenet of the Constitution by adopting a new law. Now, only 435 maximum seats are allocated regardless of the population. This of course has made them all more important and thus worthy of a large salary and expenses. In 2009, for example without unvouchered expenses, your congressman pocketed $174,000.00. Not bad for a part time job.

With a growing population, the ratio in the House of Representatives right now is about 1 in 700,000. That's an awful lot of hands to shake for just one person. So, they don't, and they know they do not have to shake anybody's hands or meet anybody. And, you don't miss them. But, you should! We get the government we deserve.

If you are good at math, you'll be able to tell this puzzle isn't over yet. Take the twenty-some mostly permanent staff members for each of the 435 representatives and multiply that (about 22) by 435 and add that to the 435 representatives. The number approaches 10,000. With the approximate U.S. citizen population just over 300,000,000 (technically illegal aliens have no representation), it can be argued that the ratio of 1 to 30,000 has magically been maintained, if you're happy talking to an aide instead of your representative.

Why they need 22 or 23 staff members is an enigma I will let hang for another day. The point is that we actually need about 9500 more Congressional Representatives to comply with the Constitution. That would certainly make our representatives much more accountable and maybe we would actually be able to reach them and maybe they would even live in our communities instead of behind gates in secret communities.

And, of course they would not be so "important and honorable," which would be good for the people. It would be a bummer for the Congressman, however, not being quite as important, but so what? Remember, we get the government we deserve.

There are lots of other sound arguments for this notion postured at the Jacksonian party blog at:

http://thejacksonianparty.spaces.live.com/blog/cns!3E751362FDD59519!143.entry

Our benign oligarchy can use a dose of direct democracy

You may choose to read more about the forms of government in the Civics Lesson included in Chapter 5. In this lesson you will learn why our form of government is known as a representative constitutional democracy. Instead of every person having a say in every decision, we elect representatives and we hold them accountable through the Constitution to make sure they don't hijack the government.

When a government is of the rich, for the rich, and by the rich, we would call that an oligarchy--rule by the few over the many. Substitute special interests for "rich," and it means the same. As long as we get no representation from our elected, we really do not have a functioning representative democracy. In practice it is an oligarchy and this is very dangerous.

As long as the oligarchy is benign, there is not much reason to be concerned other than that long before the year 2000, the government was already hijacked and still nobody is calling anybody on it. The great insights of Dr. Michael Savage, a well-known syndicated Radio Talk Show Host suggest that the time to get really worried about your free speech is when the few begin sending out the big black cars and one at a time, the many begin to disappear into the gulags.

Back when the big issues began in 2010, it seemed as if the Obama Czars all came equipped with questionable integrity and a tailor made government hijacking kit. Watch out. We elected Trump to remove the czars. Are they gone? We get the government we deserve.

In a Direct Democracy, the people have the vote, not the representatives, and this type of democracy is based on the principles of Initiation, Referendum, and Recall. Many of the states of the union also have these notions in their constitutions, but our founding fathers believed at the time that the checks and balances they built into the early government would permit the constitutional democracy (Republic) to last for quite a long time.

They originally thought that professionals, such as our Senators, one from each state, would be the proper way to run the country. As the Articles of Confederation were woven into the Constitution, this notion changed to two senators per state, not elected directly by the people but by the state legislatures, and a House of Representatives of the people, elected directly by the people.

Checks and balances aren't working

As they say at realdemocracy.com, "DEMOCRACY WON'T WORK UNLESS YOU FIND THE TRUTH AND KEEP YOURSELF INFORMED." Stay ignorant of how things really are and you will almost certainly reap the government you deserve.

The checks and balances of the Founding Fathers include (1) the Constitution itself, and (2) the three "equal" branches of government. But the big trick they had up their sleeves was that the (3) representatives in the House were elected, not appointed and there was a huge electorate to make sure that bad representatives would not be reelected.

In other words, the founders believed that the American people would weed out the bad guys so that the bad guys could not corrupt the government. These three notions were intended to keep the representatives of the government serving the people and not serving special interests. If this were the case in practice, however, I would not have been challenged to write this book.

Our representatives have failed us and they unfortunately, are the most direct means of solving the problem. But, why will they? Good question! It always comes down to un-electing stubborn representatives who refuse to do the will of the people. Most people don't have the guts because something might happen to their nephews who hold government jobs. We get the government we deserve. If only others must sacrifice to clean up government, it will remain dirty.

Since the government is beginning to behave as an oligarchy and this was never the intention of the Founding Fathers as they drafted the Constitution, an injection of Direct Democracy might just be what the doctor ordered. It is fully in line with our U.S. Constitution, which vests ultimate sovereignty in the people, to create a mechanism that would permit the people back into our government process.

Our corrupt representatives have taken the people out of our democracy and some direct democracy principles can reinsert the people into the scenario.

Through a constitutional amendment, for example, the people could gain the right to initiate national legislation (Initiative), create national referenda (Referendum), or demand the recall of officials (nowadays called scoundrels), who do not represent the people (Recall).

When the amendment passes, these activities could be sponsored by various public groups, or through the local and state governments. These three pillars of a direct democracy are presently reserved for the states whose constitutions specify these rights. It would be a relatively minor addition to our political system to engage the public in having a role in setting the political agenda. With how far our corrupt representatives have hijacked our national government, the time to act is now. We get the government we deserve.

Unfortunately, as noted above, not even all states have constitutions which permit the three prongs of a direct democracy. For example, my home state of Pennsylvania, has no statewide initiative or referendum rights, though Philadelphia and Allegheny (Pittsburgh) counties have it at the local level.

A group of Pennsylvanians called the "PA Taxpayers for Referendum Organization" are planning legislation to create a state constitutional convention to give PA these important rights. Many notable historical figures have suggested that our representative constitutional democracy could be improved with Initiative and Referendum. Their reasons seem to fit the national mood and the national need.

Theodore Roosevelt, for example, in his "Charter of Democracy" speech of 1912 said, "I believe in the initiative and referendum, which should be used not to destroy representative government, but to correct it whenever it becomes misrepresentative." Abraham Lincoln is well known for his words, "Government is of the people, for the people and by the people." Referendum is recall of government if the government does not act in a responsible way.

Back in 2005, the League of Women Voters of Pennsylvania took heed and offered that it "believes that citizens should have some means of taking direct action if their elected representatives fail to enact laws that voters support, or if they pass laws that are not wanted by the people." Does any of this hit home?

Whether at the state level or the federal level, any thought of the public as a whole being able to participate in the political agenda, with majority rule and one-vote-one-value, would send shivers down the spine of political operatives. The corporate owned corrupt media would go nuts. It would even appear to be a menace to all minority groups who today exercise disproportionate power through representatives.

But, fear not. As you know the Irish are a minority and I am Irish. The Catholics are a minority, and I am Catholic. As minority groups, this change would affect both of these groups, but maybe that is OK and for the greater good. I don't have a problem with the notion at all. It would actually be a way of controlling the idea often referred to as the tyranny of the minority in which the voice of a few have disproportionate power to their numbers over the many.

Watch Your Words; The Media 'll Get You

Elitists in the media and the bureaucracy who claim the right to know what's best for us every day pour forth a deluge of abuse and character assassination arguments to keep "We the People" in our place. In the 2008 presidential election, for example, the media anointed Senator McCain as the winner of the GOP nomination after Super Tuesday, though my state, Pennsylvania, and many other states had yet to express their opinions on the matter.

These volleys and even attacks don't come from nowhere. They come from the power-packed corporatocracy that owns the corrupt media. Watch what they say a little more carefully if you please, because they slander anybody who disagrees with them or who can alter their grip on power and propaganda. Though I believe that John McCain was a better choice than John McCain, I have learned enough about McCain since then that I feel his presidency would not have achieved many greater results. John McCain is no Donald Trump.

In a 2018 book, such as this, we should not be talking about John Edwards but we all learn from history. Some think that John Edwards' story and how he was summarily removed from the primary elections right from the beginning is actually a case study for the abuse of corporate power. When the powerful do not like somebody who is imperfect, they know how to slither in a less-capable person and they know how to make the terrible seem like Superman. You and I cannot pay for the ads needed to do that.

Edwards, though selfishly motivated was a real champion against the established corporate power chieftains. He was a kick-butt trial lawyer who ate corporate chieftains for breakfast and salted away a huge nest egg of Kabul-licks for himself. He was defamed by the corporation-owned media simply because he was a "nasty" trial-lawyer. The real reason was that he was a threat to their livelihood. a

The irony is that the Democratic Party was and is still in bed with the trial lawyers. They wanted nothing to do with Edwards' promises to end the problems of "greedy corporations." Media surrogates instantly plopped the "trial-lawyer" label on Edwards and he was gone even before Super Tuesday.

Since the election of course, we all learned a few more leaked sordid details about John Edwards to make us feel good that corporate America destroyed him. but perhaps we were the people duped before Super Tuesday by the corrupt media? We get the government we deserve.

As you will note in Chapter 12, corporations are a huge threat to our democracy and they need to be toned down a good measure so that real little guys do not feel their sting and so companies, such as General Electric do not have undue influence on our lives through their media holdings.

Way back in 2009, Forbes declared GE as the largest corporation in the world. There was a time that GE controlled NBC and MSNBC and CNBC. This level of control gave the corporate behemoth a little more influence on American life than is good for the people.

The Brave New World

Note: http://en.wikipedia.org/wiki/Brave_New_World,

Aldous Huxley wrote the <u>Brave New World</u> as a novel in 1932. The book is about the future and its setting is London, 2540 A.D. The novel anticipates that all of the reproductive advancements that today are just notions in a lab someplace, including biological engineering, and sleep-learning, will be commonplace in the future and will be used to change society. The book talks about drug use as pacifiers to make the people feel better and loudspeakers used to get across the message. Later Huxley wrote two other books on the topic, one thirty years later in which he saw the future coming much sooner and the other, The Island, which took the sterile notions of Brave New World and made them more attractive and more positive. For example, loudspeakers are replaced by pleasing parrots trained to offer uplifting slogans.

Is our current day, " the Brave New World revisited," is a new deal in which the Government hands out pacifiers to keep the citizenry in a state of euphoria? What does such euphoria look like?

For the politician, it is a no-cost notion since they get elected by bribing you with your own money. Many citizens want there to be "no problems" so much so that they can't or won't listen to hear that there actually is a big problem that requires them to pay for its solution.

Yet, that is the system we have. Politicians who speak the truth are rejected because the voting public would rather be served denial and sugar and some pacifying stimuli. Ask Aldous Huxley, if you can find him.

Some people think Trump is the devil, but their facts are flimsy. I tend to think of Trump as an imperfect person who wishes he were a better man and who is hell-bent on becoming one. Sometimes we have to go back to know how close we were as a country to losing our identity.

Very early in the 2008 primaries we saw the media at work with sugar packets for those of us that don't mind being fat and Splenda for the slender among us. The media early on picked John McCain and Hillary Clinton as the only viable candidates. They just as quickly and amazingly switched to Barack Obama, though they owed Hillary and they knew it.

The media, and the Independents took the Republican primary from the Republicans without a whimper and they brought their man McCain in from sure doom to be the Republican Primary victor. Somehow, they found a faux conservative in the lot and that's what the Republicans got by going along to get along.

The utterly corrupt corporate media, the low ratings media I might add, helped voters come to the media way of thinking with a constant barrage of propaganda for their guys and against all the others. The sinister part of the deal is that the propaganda sounded a lot like hard news. Intrinsically we all know that there is no free lunch but "don't ask me to pay!" We get the government we deserve.

Could we stomach the change we need?

Both parties each election spend more and more money to get elected then, while in office because they get rewarded for spending our money, they get reelected, which is reward enough. Even the Republican Party, though much more honest than the utterly corrupt

Democrats, were big spenders during the Bush years. What was that all about?

Republicans and Democrats of course do not want to pay for spending with taxes, which affect their reelection opportunities, so they borrow and the poor, those on social security, the middle class and the rest of America pay the price by suffering with inflation.

The Democrats can always get a little more from the rich by implicitly invoking the subtle principles of class warfare. Both parties seem to have no problem borrowing from and bankrupting Social Security, which was supposed to have been in an Al Gore style, Lock Box.

Nobody talks about it because it serves no politician well, but the biggest tax is the inflation this spending behavior causes. There was no bigger spender in history than Barack Obama and his team of czars. Ironically, inflation is the worst and heaviest tax on the working poor. Each year, more Americans fall below the living wage because we pay for government's excessive spending with inflation and not taxes. Taxes were already high enough, but somebody had to pay for political pork (porkulus) and you know it would not be the politicians or the ruling class.

Each year the shrinking middle class fakes its standard of living by borrowing more, the only sensible thing when you have inflation. Greed of the ruling political class finished the Roman Empire and it is well lined up to finish the American economic empire. "Free healthcare" was almost been the final Obama-era nail in the US coffin.

Until the healthcare debate of 2009, I did not have overly high hopes that the electorate would opt to change anything as long as they too got something that benefitted them in the notion of "someone else will pay politics." The revolt of the summer of 2009 that has continued tells me that the people now seem more interested in the US as a surviving entity as any other issue I have ever seen.

The free lunch in 2018 is over folks. Until Barack Obama caricaturized government largesse with free-fall spending like never before, it seemed like many Americans, getting by barely, stubbornly were hanging on, sending back the political hacks for two more years or four more years or six more years, even when they chose not to represent us.

The sun seems to be shining on this folly now as more and more people are crying to throw the bums out. Trump was elected to eliminate a whole SWAMP of people. If he can, lots of normal people will cheer.

This downslide must end. It won't end, however, until we choose to end it at the ballot box and we forever hold the lesser "honorables" accountable or better yet, we just send them home to get real jobs like the rest of us.

The question always was, "do we have the stomach to do what is right?" Your friendly neighborhood politicians, all the way to the lords of the national ring are banking that you and I don't have the guts to do it. This time, I think they are wrong. We already brought Trump in at the top of the government.

The sleeping giants have been awakened. Americans are ready to fight another revolution to take America back. Perhaps we are not ready, but I think we are. Either way, we get the government we deserve.

Shall we cast off what is left of our independence and join the major political parties and ask for more government control and then we can loudly applaud our political leaders at important reelection functions? Maybe we can carry around their nominating petitions, and even hand out how-to-vote cards at elections.

Or, should we clamp down on this big problem with our democracy, speak up, demand action, and if we are not satisfied, now really, shouldn't we just throw the bums out?

Democracy is a relatively new phenomenon in its modern forms. It has developed over the last few centuries to a somewhat acceptable level in perhaps 40 of the world's 200-odd nation states. Judging from the U.S., it must further evolve. It cannot remain fixed in the face of accelerating change in all other aspects of society and the outright threat of takeover by corporate power and influence or as John Edwards correctly characterized it, "corporate greed."

The elements of direct democracy such as Initiative, Referendum, and Recall are anathema to politicians and governments at all levels. Yet, all three of these tenets could help enliven the political experience for the people and make government at all levels more accountable. In all western democracies, including the good ole U.S. of A., there are high levels of dissatisfaction.

Thus, there is more and more interest in politics by the yet-to-be-disillusioned young and things that can improve politics such as the Initiative amendment need to be brought forth and adopted. The mood of the country, voiced often by the young in the past presidential election brought forth the current administration and now the American people are getting changes many had never considered possible and every day it seems there is more.

The Bush years brought great division over the war in Iraq and a very unpopular president, from his own doing along with the help of the corrupt, left leaning media. So, now, we have trillions of dollars of debt, give-away programs for the rich (Wall street and the Bankers) that are better than PowerBall, and a big war in in the Middle East that until Mad Dog Mattis showed up did not seem to be fought well.

We also have a CIA that was being emasculated and politicized, and we seem to have no fear at all of terrorism as the name during the former president's administration was even stricken from the federal dictionary. It seems that Michele and Barack had begun to live with Alice and the Tin Man to not notice that the America they shepherded was crumbling. On top of the new stuff, there is still the same old deep division in this country about open borders, the full response to terrorism, and the ongoing Iraq and Afghanistan wars. I fear these are just a few symptoms of a much deeper malaise. Thankfully for now, President Trump has these all on his agenda.

Familiarity Breeds Contempt

People everywhere seem to want to push the bounds of democracy further than their governments will allow. Both Prime Minister Blair in the UK and President Bush in the U.S. in their day, led incredibly unpopular governments. But, they are of the past and new guys eventually took their places.

Gordon Brown got off to a great start as the #1 in the UK and our own Barack Obama was so popular he was almost declared a King and ruler for life in America until the 2016 election. Americans actually loved everything about the Obama family, from the kids to the new dog.

Never have I seen such a high level of satisfaction for any President. Brits, sick of Tony Blaire and the Iraq War, were likewise quite pleased with Gordon Brown, though not at the level of the American love affair. Congratulations to both for their fine early showings. Those days too are gone as are Obama and Gordon Brown.

In addition to the big new rap of fiscal irresponsibility, the dissatisfaction with the U.S. government at all levels stems from many reasons such as a steady slide in social, economic and environmental conditions in the past 20 years; the increasingly overt nepotism, careerism, cronyism and outright corruption in our political system and in the government, itself.

Who do you trust? What once was a Johnny Carson game show tease, is now a question that beckons to be answered well but seemingly cannot be. In 2009, more and more blog contributions were asking, "Do you trust your government?"

On top of a major dislike for having unpopular notions rammed down the public's collective throat, much of this is fueled by public revulsion at brain-numbing political campaigns, the blatant disregard for the public in official decision-making, the dominance of big business, big unions, and big government, the flaunting of wealth by the ruling class, and increasingly fat salaries for politicians.

Meanwhile the general public (that's us) is chopped liver, theoretically living beyond its means, and we all have no recourse but to work harder for less money. With the economic collapse of late 2008, living beyond ones means has actually taken on new meaning and many individuals have been forced to follow this mantra.

Not to be outdone, the Federal government finds no need at all to have a balanced checkbook, and those trying to balance theirs find it a bit disingenuous of our politicians to take pay raises while they are systematically draining the US treasury for their pet reelection projects. Is Nero fiddling again?

We the people have to tighten our belts to compete with those foreigners who would take our jobs while living either legally or illegally in the U.S., as well as those who would be pleased to do their jobs in China, India, or Russia or a host of developing nations. It's not pretty on the streets. " Let them eat cake" seemed to be the government response until the new Trump Administration. .

The public in ever increasing numbers, is also recognizing the structural defects of its political system. The centralization of power within the major parties so that there is no longer a two-party system nor room for independents is becoming quite obvious. Bush, Clinton, Bush, Clinton was almost not just a bad joke; it was almost a reality. Former president Barack Obama benefited on that one.

Add to all of this bad stuff the negativism and personal abuse inherent in adversary partisan politics, the domination of public decision-making by small elites, major party collusion depriving the public of choice, an institutionalized "broken promise syndrome," the failure of the government to be able to handle organized minority groups--legal and illegal--and undemocratic electoral systems and machines where only by chance, and sometimes in spite of devious manipulation, does the resulting government reflect the will of the people.

When representatives of the government from the Democrat Party call citizens at Town Hall meetings Astroturfers, and disingenuous, and at the same time they send their bought and paid for thugs and operatives (yes, the operatives of our legislators vs. the people) to combat and disrupt the "undue influence" of John Q Public on the fair and open legislative process, isn't this really an awful ugly pot calling the kettle names. Did anybody mention the words "healthcare," and "government control?"

In a democracy, it is axiomatic that the majority can only govern with the consent of the minority. Yet it helps to have a majority. Our last set of presidential elections show that there is a deep divide in this country. Yet until Trump, the good old boys in Congress (The SWAMP) sought bipartisan labels for their "solutions." It makes no sense since the biggest problem may just well be the political parties that breed our representatives.

The fact that the Democrats cannot accept defeat and have conjured up a number of faux methods to convince the people that their elected president is illegitimate is simply outrageous and un-American. Nobody but a Democrat likes a sore loser.

The new Congress seems to never be able to consider electoral matters except in terms of their partisan advantage. Underlying the alienation and powerlessness people feel is the lack of a true representative democracy, the accelerating rate of change since the 1980s, the information revolution, the forces of corporate globalization and the ongoing tyranny of the minorities. And they were the good ole days.

Chapter 4 Life for Politicians Will Never Be the Same

Poor representation may be worse than none

Today, as we now have a president with about a year under his belt, and as a country we got the change we asked for, the rift is still huge. And though the above underlying principles and all of the symptoms of no representation that once existed still exist, the debate to many has gotten even more personal.

It has shifted from just plain old poor and often corrupt representation to a new and deep concern that the actions or inaction (lack of reading legislation and voting for it as an example) of the elected may change the nature of the country forever.

Whether it is a fear of full-bore socialism, or a fear of giving up one's whole paycheck or one's own healthcare to get just a piece of it back, the people have been awakened and life for politicians will never be the same. And, that is good.

But the politicians will not take this sitting down. Will they actually consider taking over the country to keep the will of the people in check?   We'll talk about this and many other things as we ponder about whether the people will get the government they deserve. Perhaps the people need to work to deserve better!

Elites Are No Longer Elite

In 1774 the English Whig Party member and Political philosopher Edmund Burke offered that representatives should be elected to govern rather than the people directly. Burke saw that such representatives should exercise their superior wisdom and judgment irrespective of the wishes of the electorate. The electorate in Burke's eyes would be easily characterized as "We the People." He saw their governance as being aided by an elitist private service -- not a public service.

For Burke, that was not only OK but highly desirable. He believed that the public would always reject the "necessary hard decisions," and thus would be incapable of meaningful governance. Today we would call him naive but back then, there appeared to have been a substantially higher level of integrity in the political class, thereby making his ideas more acceptable for the times.

Many, including the framers of our Constitution were influenced by Burke, but the elitists envisioned by Burke in his writings were not greedy politicians and corporate profiteers who also happened to be wealthy. For Burke, the elitists were in fact the elite of society, the cream of the crop—the good of society—by all standards.

They were people you would like if you met them. They were not pretentious. They just happened to be better schooled and in many ways more intelligent and more capable of grappling through the tough decisions. They were not the greedy knaves who hold office on our behalf today.

The overall Edmund Burke philosophy is no longer acceptable to a vast number of people, though it is still promulgated by elitist editorialists, bureaucrats and some academicians. The problem with this notion is the tacit acceptance of an indefinable inequality and the fact that the good unquoted elite can very easily become members of the bad "elite," a group who are well characterized by taking substantially more than they give back. The bad elite have an aka they should resent—the SWAMP!

No Secrets!

The more eyes that look at the machinations of government, the safer and more prosperous we all will be. There are many arguments against open government at all levels, but history tells us that secrecy is a formula for corruption and long-term failure. Additionally, secrecy in government all too often provides for the perpetrators to avoid the responsibility and accountability that would be required if their actions were well known.

The fact is that corruption scandals are regular occurrences in governments across the world, and as you examine these failings, secrecy is always a required ingredient. If government is not always open, then what is it? Closed? If it is truly closed then how is it that in this closed scenario, the secret decision-making is always known by a privileged few who profit from the knowledge?

Watch to see if Jeffrey Immelt, CEO of GE, world's largest corporation, formerly director of message for NBC and MSNBC before GE unloaded them, does not get to enrich his company through some secret deals with his new buddy, President Barack Obama. Obama, the claimed champion of the little guy, in his inner chambers had room for people of all backgrounds, including corporate profiteers and plain ole filthy rich people. The former president was a gamer who know where the real power emanated.

Watch closely to see if there are any rewards to Immelt of GE for being in on the secret meetings which do not occur. It is intuitive that in a closed government, only John Doe and Jane Q. Public are kept in the dark. Somehow, speculators would bet that Jeffrey Immelt gets the full lighted treatment. As open as our government is on paper, secret meetings are commonplace. Thus, we must be wary since these closed sessions occur with "our" representatives at all levels. When they are out of sight in secrecy, we can bet that they are representing somebody other than "We the People."

With an educated populace as exists in the 21st century, it is in fact dangerous to merely trust our representatives with our government. We can be assured that they will not do the right thing. We must, as Ronald Reagan would say "trust but verify." It is all too easy for elected representatives and even their minions, the bureaucrats, to assume that a shroud of wisdom comes down on them once they have arrived in their office.

It is so much easier to serve the private rather than the public interest when dressed in the veil of secrecy, steering clear of accountability. Without a doubt, our most recent history furnishes abundant proof. Open the shades and bring in the light of day. Open the windows, please, and let the stink out of the room--for good. We get the government we deserve.

Summary

The Representative Democracy that our forefathers brought to this country is not functioning properly. Our elected representatives at all levels of government view the notion of representatives in a much more opportunistic way than intended by the Constitution. To solve this problem, we must admit that government is out of control and no longer is of the people, for the people, and by the people, and we must have the guts to correct it, even if it means not getting something for ourselves from the largesse pile.

The time to fix it is now, perhaps before those really in charge become aware of their full power and we never have the opportunity again to gain control. The time is now. We get the government we deserve.

Chapter 5 The Tax "Cuts" of 2017

Republicans could not count on Republicans

It took them about a full year to do, but both the Republican-Controlled House & Senate finally got together and passed a comprehensive tax reform bill. They promised a simple bill and a simplified tax code but that did not happen. Nonetheless, the bill that President Trump signed into law on Friday, December 22, 2017 was a "sweeping Republican tax legislation. It went down as Trump's first major legislative accomplishment since winning the White House.

During the signing celebration, the President spoke at length. He first thanked the ineffectual Republicans in Congress for finally getting some legislation to his desk and then the President predicted that would help the economy substantially.

"It's going to be a tremendous thing for the American people. It's going to be fantastic for the economy," Trump told reporters in the Oval Office. "It's going to keep companies from leaving our shores and opening up in other countries."

Trump said the decision to sign the bill on Friday was made late and because of criticism in the press that it was being delayed.

As a result, Trump was not surrounded by the congressional leaders who after getting nothing done for a full-year, had shepherded the tax bill to him. He even offered the pens to reporters which would usually have been given to those members of Congress.

Trump said he was originally going to wait to sign the bill in a formal ceremony in January, but the media was asking if he would sign it before Christmas as he had pledged.

"I am keeping my promise," he said. "I am signing it before Christmas."

Trump noted that a number of companies have announced bonuses and new investment because of the legislation. He added that "Corporations are literally going wild over this," he said.
Trump touted various aspects of the plan, including the larger standard deduction, the increase in the amount exempt from the estate tax and the repatriation of earnings that companies currently have held overseas.

The bill's signing ended the president's first year in office on a very high note.

President Trump had been calling for tax cuts since the early days of his presidential campaign. He first released a tax plan in September 2015, about three months after announcing his candidacy. The reason it took so long is that the Congress does not represent normal Americans.

The new tax law is really a winner for regular normal people though corrupt Democratic lawmakers such as Bob Casey, my Senator from Pennsylvania have lied about it from the beginning. How can a plan that lowers rates for individuals and corporations and roughly doubles the standard deduction, increases the child tax credit and curbs a number of corporate tax breaks not be viewed as a tax plan for normal Americans? I am afraid it is because for Democrats it is business as usual: "Find the truth and then lie if it hurts the Party."

Because of the way it was passed, in order to comply with Senate budget rules, the cuts for individuals expire after 2025, while the lower corporate tax rate is permanent. I would sure hope that when the country finds out the benefits of these cuts to 90% of Americans, our inept legislature will come together and make the cuts and the reforms permanent.

For the first time since the Trump election, Republicans in Congress were united throughout the tax-overhaul process. Many suspect that having no accomplishments at all was a non-starter for those Senators facing reelection in 2018. They had to show the public that they could govern after their multiple setbacks on health care. Every

GOP senator present voted for the final package, and there were only 12 defections among House Republicans. I say we get their names.

Trump publicly made efforts to try to get Democrats, who care more about themselves and the Party than the general public, to vote for the measure as well. He thought that senators facing 2018 reelection bids in states the president carried in 2016 would see the light but Democrats preferred to slam Trump's gift to America rather than get on board and support Americans. Partisan politics again ruled the Democratic Party as no Democrat in either chamber of Congress ultimately backed the package.

Democrats have focused on the fact that some taxpayers would see tax increases and have lied that that the largest benefits will go to wealthy people like the president. They used a political strategy rather than a pro-US strategy. They attacked Republicans rather than support their constituents as they believe they can lie again when the midterms since the polls conducted by the fake-news media show the Democratic talking points (known as lies to those who do fact-checks) make the bill unpopular with the public.

Republicans finally are smart and have brushed off the polls. They know that when the truth comes out, public opinion will change in February as the people start to see higher take-home pay. They argue that the bill will be a big winner because it will boost job creation, wages and the economy. Democrats, betting on a lie, are heading for a big defeat in my humble opinion.

Trump predicted that he wouldn't have to spend much time on the road selling the bill because people will be pleased with their bigger paychecks.

"I don't think I'm going to have to travel too much to sell it," he said. "I think it's selling itself."

A Democrat's perspective on taxation

Sometimes you learn the best life's lessons by simply opening your email. When I opened it this morning, it contained this treat. It clearly shows that the Democrat's way of evaluating tax reform cannot lead to long-term prosperity.

From: "BobW"
To: "'Brian"
Subject: FW: Tax System Explained and Clarified??...Enjoy!!

Suppose that every day, ten men go out for beer and the bill for all ten comes to $100.

If they paid their bill the way we pay our taxes, it would go something like this:

- ✓ The first four men (the poorest) would pay nothing.
- ✓ The fifth would pay $1.
- ✓ The sixth would pay $3.
- ✓ The seventh would pay $7.
- ✓ The eighth would pay $12.
- ✓ The ninth would pay $18.
- ✓ The tenth man (the richest) would pay $59.

So, that's what they decided to do. The ten men drank in the bar every day and seemed quite happy with the arrangement, until one day, the owner threw them a curve.

"Since you are all such good customers," he said, "I'm going to reduce the cost of your daily beer by $20. "Drinks for the ten now cost just $80.

The group still wanted to pay their bill the way we pay our taxes so the first four men were unaffected. They would still drink for free. But what about the other six men - the paying customers?

How could they divide the $20 windfall so that everyone would get his 'fair share?'

They realized that $20 divided by six is $3.33. But if they subtracted that from everybody's share, then the fifth man and the sixth man would each end up being paid to drink his beer. So, the bar owner suggested that it would be fair to reduce each man's bill by roughly the same amount, and he proceeded to work out the amounts each should pay.

And so: The fifth man, like the first four, now paid nothing (100% savings). The sixth now paid $2 instead of $3 (33%savings). The seventh now pay $5 instead of $7 (28%savings). The eighth now paid $9 instead of $12 (25% savings). The ninth now paid $14 instead of $18 (22% savings). The tenth now paid $49 instead of $59 (16% savings).

Each of the six was better off than before. And the first four continued to drink for free. But once outside the restaurant, the men began to compare their savings.

"I only got a dollar out of the $20,"declared the sixth man. He pointed to the tenth man, " but he got $10!"

"Yeah, that's right," exclaimed the fifth man. "I only saved a dollar, too. It's unfair that he got ten times more than I!"

"That's true!!" shouted the seventh man. "Why should he get $10 back then I got only two? The wealthy get all the breaks!"

"Wait a minute," yelled the first four men in unison. "We didn't get anything at all. The system exploits the poor!"

The nine men surrounded the tenth and beat him up. The next night the tenth man didn't show up for drinks, so the nine sat down and had beers without him.

But when it came time to pay the bill, they discovered something important. They didn't have enough money between all of them for even half of the bill!

And that, boys and girls, journalists and college professors, is how our tax system works. The people who pay the highest taxes get the most benefit from a tax reduction.

Tax them too much, attack them for being wealthy, and they just may not show up anymore

In fact, they might start drinking overseas where the atmosphere is somewhat friendlier

For those who understand, no explanation is needed. For those who do not understand, no explanation could ever be possible.

Chapter 6 Too Many Honorables

The Issues of Today

Something happened to representative government from the time of the Declaration of Independence and Constitution to the present. Though our representative constitutional democracy has survived for about 230 years, it is not at its healthiest right now. Here are just a few of the major problems that we are facing as a nation:

- The threat of socialism from the government
- The war on terrorism (whatever they call it now)
- Wars in Iraq and Afghanistan
- North Korean nukes & missiles
- L-1A and L-1B foreign national visas
- H-1B and D-1 foreign national visas
- Illegal immigration
- Excessive legal immigration
- Corporate power and greed
- Labor arbitrage / offshoring
- Jobs
- Election process corruption
- Healthcare availability and affordability
- Obamacare
- Institution of marriage
- Respect for life
- Influence of special interests
- Lobbying
- Private property confiscation
- Political and corporate corruption
- Energy and oil
- Homeland security
- Social Security
- Student loan debt

- Free trade
- Tax reform
- Economy
- Education
- Crime / drugs / gangs

No book can attack all of these issues (listed in no specific order) and be substantive enough to be informative. So, this book concentrates on the elements of taxation and our lack of representation on all fronts. It focuses on the ability to earn a living and the trouble with corporations as non-equal equal citizens, labor issues, foreign nationals, illegal immigration, and labor arbitrage / offshoring.

The book also takes a look at controversial election laws designed to facilitate fraud for the good of the two party system at the expense of We the People. There are more than enough topics in this abbreviated list for us to examine and offer possible solutions. We'll have to leave the rest to our elected representatives.

Our congressional representatives, and presidential representatives (yes, even the president is supposed to administer the will of the people) have to deal with all of the issues in the big list above as well as others. In 2008, while in the midst of the presidential campaigns, through all sorts of media and the Internet, Americans were able to see what the potential presidential representatives thought about these issues and what they would do to "change" things for the better if they could sell us on putting them in office. Change certainly was the theme in 2008's presidential primaries and it continued into the general election. Now, many who sought change in 2008, 2012, are had buyers' remorse in 2016.

Along the way, we even learned from Mitt Romney that not only was Washington broke, it was broken and needed quick, yet lasting repair. Now, after eight years of Obama, it is even more broke and broken as the Obama fix came right out of Carl Marx's playbook. .

Promises, promises, promises. How can you tell when a politician is lying? The comic answer of course is, "when their lips are moving." That's because there is a big difference in the spoken words of politicians prior to the election and after being elected. Let me tell a short story to make my point. When we talk about the man who once tied for best presidential orator of all time with Bill Clinton, former president Barack Obama, the word is, don't even listen to what he says, watch what he does. If I were a comedian, I might suggest that only his teleprompter ever knew for sure.

After saying he was not a politician, former president Obama was the worst kind. He had a tough time with the truth. The same goes for our promising politicians. During the election process they sell, sell, sell using the level of promises necessary to convince the public. Lies are their modus operandi.

Nobody on the campaign team can say anything negative about the candidate or a proposed solution to an issue even if it is true. If you can't get a promise from a politician on the campaigning side, you more than likely will not get one when they are elected. Renege is another favorite technique of our elected representatives. Once elected, all bets are off; and the truth and facts and real intentions take over.

Unfortunately for the American people, when politicians as legislators choose not to fulfill the essence of their promises, we cannot send them back home right away. We cannot assess a penalty for lying to us about their real intentions. We do have initiative, referendum, and recall at the state level but not at the federal level. Moreover, it would take a groundswell and an act of congress (literally) to make that work. Congress has continually chosen not to discipline itself. So we wind up being stuck with politicians instead of being supported by our elected representatives.

The Honorable Congressman from Blankety Blank

Then what? Then we have to treat them like gold and call them "the honorable so and so from such and such." We must always be wary that they do not hurt us too bad. Somehow in the last fifty years and perhaps longer, the notion of the representative as a noble person as in "nobility" has been creeping into our etiquette. Yet, not only are most politicians dishonorable, they are corrupt, and they do not represent the people once elected. We know who they represent—special interests, corporations, and the ruling class of elite citizens.

They tax us and tax us and tax us, but they do not represent us. This is clearly taxation without representation but not quite as it was before the Tea Party. The tea is brewing today in a bigger way and it is much hotter than when I wrote the first edition of this book in 2008. Just like before the original tea party, the people on the streets are getting more and more riled about this.

Originally it was the young and they elected Barack Obama as their savior. Now it is everybody and before his departure, Obama became part of the problem, not the solution.

The young have surely become more active in the election process. For example, without using these words, the first meaning of their buzzword "change" is "Throw the Bums Out!" And, for how "the honorables" they have treated us when given the privilege to represent us, they are worse than bums, indeed.

Even the young did not expect Obama to be more like Mayor Daly than Abraham Lincoln. And the seniors, they think that the change they asked for was just, "no more Bush." Then, they found the new guy, Obama was ready to deny them SSR increases and also ready to steal their healthcare to pay for somebody else's healthcare.

The lack of representation is a big problem for regular Americans, young and old, and it manifests itself in legislation or lack of legislation to protect even our most basic rights. Among their despicable acts, our representatives have tried to give our healthcare to 50,000,000 more potential voters, given our jobs to legal foreign nationals, have permitted greedy American corporations to swindle stockholders and employees and to take American jobs overseas, and they have permitted illegal foreign nationals to settle permanently in the U.S. to take our jobs and take our tax money.

Then, to add insult to injury, our former president as well as the Congress have told us that we don't really want our jobs or our own healthcare and that all of this charade is good for America. Phooey!

Chapter 7 Use Scientific Method to Solve "Honorables" Problem

Scientific Method is used for problem solving

Problems that can be solved fit nicely in a notion called *The Scientific Method of Problem Solving*. The idea is to know the problem, come up with some solutions, test the solutions, and then draw conclusions from the observations and testing. The problem, which I would like to tackle using the scientific method is that representative government is not working, and it needs to be fixed.

Unfortunately, that topic is too big for this chapter and it is addressed throughout this book. But, we can attack a more discrete subset of the issue and we can have some fun at the same time.

The problem for today is that we the people honor despicable politicians with large titles though they do not deserve them -- and of course this contributes to the lack of representation. Analyzing and posturing solutions to this problem about our leaders will both enlighten and amuse as we walk through its solving via the Scientific Method.

The Scientific Method deals with problems, not symptoms. A runny nose, for example, is a symptom of a problem. The problem may be a cold, the H1N1 flu, or perhaps an allergy. For argument's sake, let's say a problem is *a real issue that can be solved by the scientific method*.

It can be defined as a question to be considered, solved, or answered. It may also be a difficult situation, matter, or person. On the lighter side, a problem may also be a misgiving, an objection, or even a complaint. A symptom, on the other hand is a *characteristic sign or manifestation of some underlying pathology*. That pathology is most often the problem.

The six basic steps in the scientific method are as follows:

1. **State the Problem** - No problem can be solved if it is not identified. In a nutshell, the problem we are exploring in this iteration is that that representatives at all levels of government, no longer represent the people from which they were elected. Moreover, they are emboldened by the honorable titles given them for merely holding office. This undue tribute affirms the pitiful work of the representative as being acceptable.

The more powerful the representative, the more toxic the effect of this callous disregard. Representatives have created their own class of people, which is a notch to many notches above the common person on the street. A root cause of this is that representatives of the people in all levels of government enjoy the adulation that comes with the office they hold... in fact they enjoy it too much.

They enjoy the separation from the hoi polloi and the sense of nobility they gain by praise and extra respect. The public feeds this notion by granting them such titles as the "Honorable" as is frequently done in Britain and, which was part of British politics at the time of the Revolutionary War. Because of the Colonists disdain for the notion of the "Nobility," the Constitution expressly forbids the granting of such titles unless authorized by Congress:

The Congress is expressly forbidden to grant titles of nobility or permit federal officials to accept gifts or titles without Congress's consent

The lawyers have probably all focused on the words, "***without Congress's consent,***" as a viable loophole, whereas the people well recognize the intent of the founding fathers.

When elected to public office, the pomp and circumstance that begins at the inauguration starts a process that sets the newly elected on a path far different from mere mortals. It is clearly irrevocable and for the rest of the politician's life, the "notion of once-elected" clearly sets them apart from those they represent or once represented.

If it weren't for the laws keeping them in the territory of their constituencies, surely, they would be able to find their just segregation. Thankfully, there are rich neighborhoods in almost every election district and the rich and well-to-do people in those neighborhoods are also "of the people." Thus, the new politician has the opportunity to find new friends of proper status so as not to have to mingle with the common electorate.

Is This Bad Behavior?

Today's finest psychologists who are always quick to find a "rational" explanation for all bad behavior might suggest that there is nothing wrong with politicians finding elite rather than humble companions worthy of fraternization. Why should a politician for example, once elected, have to break bread with a plumber, an electrician, a computer programmer, a salad tosser, or a hamburger flipper when there are people with fountains of money in their pockets and a taste for powerful friends?

Hyperbole and oversimplification aside, there is no doubt that in general, the rich and the powerful have perennially been consenting bedfellows to politicians, a symbiosis that leaves nary a crumb for the toiling paeans who bake their very bread.

It is proper and even dutiful to now ask. "Are our representatives in government excessively elevated and exalted?" This singular question expands into many. Do they quickly begin to exhibit a sense of self-importance and arrogance upon accepting their office as in the case of the infamous *pompous* politician?

Or by virtue of their office, have they in fact become magnificent, illustrious, of great renown, deserving and entitled to honor? Does the praise and high respect given even the newly elected arise because it testifies to their creditable conduct or their consistent untarnished reputation?

Does it mean that intuitively at the end of the oath, and at the end of the day (a phrase very popular for politicians today) they have become guided by a high sense of honor and duty, characterized by a massive gob of ... well, let's just say it ... integrity?

Or is Nero Caesar alive, healthy, and among us? Surely these are all good questions and I think you know on which side of the argument our esteemed psychologists would find our esteemed politicians.

If there were something wrong with all of these compliments attributing the finest attributes of a person to our political class, surely, the psychologists would have identified it and would already be correcting it. But, why does the proletariat accept all of this pomposity from its representatives as if it is the only way it should be? I would answer the last question by suggesting that Jane Q. Public does not spend a lot of time on the question.

If Jane Q. spent the time required to analyze what this is all about, she would more than likely conclude that it is nothing more than innocuous puffery. She would see that it serves to ingratiate the representative to be more inclined to offer benefits to the represented who offer such tributes. The bottom line for Jane Q. and quite frankly for John Q. also is that they would let it happen because there appears to be no harm done.

Should We Care?

Being a John Q. myself and knowing lots of other John Q's, I must admit that the puffery is getting old to many of us and you the reader are now included in our lot. This book in many ways is about the effects such puffery has on the laws and the enforcement of laws in this country.

We are not talking about the emperor and his new clothes since the constituency of ourselves, unless feeling direct pain from the hand of a politician, do not even look to see the emperor unmasked or unclothed as "hizzoner." Basically we do not care about the platitudes given and we give them sometimes ourselves, though with misgivings.

Does this attitude of honoring the "Honorables" because it is what everybody does, hurt John Q.? In a word, "Yes" it does, because this flattery, harmless as it may be given, does inflate the political ego and thus creates more separation of the representatives from the represented. It does not promote the common good. Additionally, it can be argued that it prompts the political class to care more for themselves and other elites than for the man on the street. And, my dear readers, that means that John Q. is really not being represented in our government today.

As you will read in further chapters of this book, our forefathers could not stand the notion of taxation without representation. If the truth be known, they could not stand any notion imposed on the subjects of the Crown, without representation from those imposed upon agreeing to such imposition.

To show their disdain for a non-representative government with the power to enforce taxation, colonial Americans chose to fight a war to gain the right to their most important demand, representative government. Using other terms, the founding fathers called this government of the people, for the people, and by the people. Unfortunately for America, many of our elected were not in history class the day this theory was explained.

This right in many ways is being squandered today by ordinary citizens who think that politicians are more than who they are. The political class in many ways is viewed by the people as if they are the ruling class and the people are their subjects. This is a bit like one would expect from a constitutional monarchy or an oligarchy, not from a democracy.

Hopefully this book and the words of others will help the people of this nation remember that we run the country and that the politicians, once elected must become public officials. To the extent we permit them to remain as politicians with some public duties, we remain unrepresented. The next election has nothing to do with the duties of those currently in office, yet an incumbent never is more at work than when involved in getting re-elected.

Those Days vs. These Days

Shortly after the Revolutionary War and after the formation of our representative government, there was a problem for the constituency. Somebody had to send representatives. At the federal level, it was not too easy for a local farmer to give up his farm and head off to Washington by wagon or horseback to represent the folks back home.

Recognizing this difficulty, in appreciation for representing the constituency, the neighbors, who were not of the aristocracy but of the commonplace, tended the representative's farm and protected the household, the mom and the kids and the animals, until the hero representative would come home and resume his life. During this period of American history, the representatives were clearly honorable, but they did not demand the title.

The irony of those days compared to these days is that in those days the representatives performed for their constituency from a sense of duty.

In these days, though one cannot strike a broad negative brush on the political class or a good person will never agree to help our cause and run for office, it seems that instead of from a sense of duty, today's "politicians" go for the office from a sense of opportunity. That's about it and that is the big problem.

I can probably end the book right here but there is lots more I have to say. When one is motivated by the sense of opportunity, one's interests lie mainly in oneself. So, I could rest my case right now but I will continue since we not only need to change the notion that the governors are elite and the governed are subjects, we must convince the best and the brightest of our country to take up the yoke as in days past and do for America from a raging sense of duty, not opportunity... and not for a lifetime.

A Country of Honor

The State of Pennsylvania is not unlike the other 49 states. So, as I speak about PA, think about the similarities with the political business in your own state. Surely some who come to office come from a sense of duty and they are fine people, while others come from the draw of opportunity.

Hence, with the dismal track record of politicos from all states and the federal government, It is better for the constituency to not trust any in elected public office until given proof that such trust is well deserved. Just like your state, the state of Pennsylvania in which I have lived all but two of my years in this life, is a state with a mix of the duty class and the opportunity class.

A number of the names in the next section are people who I know from my own area of the state. As I mention names and titles, please do not draw any conclusions on the specific individuals that I mention (at least in this chapter) A number of office-holders, such as former magistrate Martin R. Kane, and William H. Amesbury from my City of Wilkes-Barre, I know are very good men.

However, I admit that I do not know all about even these two. I met Kane as he was serving as a Justice of the Peace at a wedding of a young man who was like a son to me. The Honorable Martin Kane could have easily dismissed this family's request to travel to the far corners of the county on a sunny holiday to marry them but instead, he welcomed it. Amesbury and I met in a Little League game when we both were 11 years old, and in all the years that have passed, I still haven't heard a bad word about hizzoner. I am also friends with our Mayor, Tony George and thankfully for Wilkes-Barre, he is a good person.

As many states in this wonderful nation, the state of Pennsylvania has many politicians bearing the title "The Honorable." Are they honorable? That is for their constituencies to examine and decide. It is absolutely amazing how many yeronners and heronners and hizzoners there are in all states, so I have chosen PA, my state, as my example state.

To put some names next to some of those honorable representatives, executives, and justices, permit me to use those with whom I am most familiar from a local standpoint and then pick them at random the further from my home town they get. For example, the list of honorables includes the Honorable Senator from Pennsylvania, Robert P. Casey, the Honorable Matt cartwright (U.S. House of Representatives), The Honorable Thomas Wolfe (Governor, Commonwealth of Pennsylvania), the Honorable Elisabeth J. Baker (PA State Senator), the Honorable Eddie Day Pashinski (PA State House of Representatives), the Honorable Anthony George, Mayor of Wilkes-Barre City, The Honorable Seamus McCaffrey (Pennsylvania Supreme Court Justice), The Honorable Christine Donohue (Pennsylvania Superior Court Justice), The Honorable Richard M. Hughes III, (President Judge, Luzerne County Courts -- , The Honorable Ray Cronauer (District Justice, Luzerne County), The Honorable William T. Amesbury -- Judge of the Common Pleas in Luzerne County). .

With no disrespect intended to any of the above, that is an awful lot of "Honorables" and it doesn't touch the number of hizzoners, heronners, and yeronners in just the state of Pennsylvania. If you begin a calculation based on current appointees and elected offices, the national total of the "Honorables," would be in the hundreds of thousands.

That's an awful lot of honor that is implicitly taken by this branch of the political class. Think of your own list in your own state and you are probably not surprised that this list is large and in almost all cases, except for Amesbury, I chose just one of many in the chamber who hold the same office.

So, as a major preamble to a problem statement using the scientific method, I have described the situation (problem) in adequate detail. The big problem is that there is taxation and there is not representation. Yet, somehow the "representatives" are all honorable.

The situation is quite similar to when King George III and Parliament in the 18th century directly levied taxes on the colonists and the colonists rebelled. Though outright rebellion is not necessarily right around the corner, the current set of "Honorables" need to pay attention to the mood of the people on this topic because the public mood is not very good. Those representatives who enjoy the game need to come to the realization again that the people come first.

Unlike the 18th century, however, there are living representatives. There just isn't real representation. The litmus test is whether that representation is of the people, for the people, and by the people. Take a look at the Honorable So and So's in your home state and in your locale, and ask if you're gifting them with the title of hizzoner has minimized the representation that you receive. I say yes it has in most cases and thus the problem statement for this problem using the scientific method, with due poetic license, can be written as follows:.

Completed Problem Statement - Scientific Method

The use of platitudes and pufferies to describe elected representatives diminishes their desire to represent the people and increases their desire to represent themselves, the elite and the special interest classes of the elite. It also decreases the expectation level of the constituency as they, by their own words, place their governors in a higher socio-political class and they submit as subjects to "what comes down the pike."

The next phase of the scientific method of problem solving is as follows:

2. **Form a Hypothesis** - Using the Scientific Method of problem solving, this represents a possible solution to the problem formed after gathering information about the problem. The term "research" must be properly applied here.

Can this hypothesis be as simple as an admonition to stop doing what we are doing? Stop giving puffery and stop accepting puffery. Is it that simple? Yes it is; but there are some other issues that we need to discuss and these follow:

From henceforth, let the representatives serve as unsung and humble heroes about whom songs of distinction will rarely be raised unless the distinction is truly earned. Let them represent the people and nobody else. Let their inner selves guide their votes and let their inner selves give them praise for jobs well done. Let the pomposity and the arrogance end and end quickly.

Puffery leads to improper allegiances

Let no special interests be permitted anywhere close to the hallowed chambers of our government and the buildings in which the business of the people is conducted. Keep the lobbyists and those backed by the money of the unknown, including that of the enemies of these United States, from the legislators (our representatives) as they are making laws for the common good of the states and the people therein.

Lobbyists and those whose income depends on influencing America's lawmakers should be permitted no contact with the representatives of the states, or any local constituency. Such activity in proximity of lawmakers is not for the common good and the lobbyist crowd should not be permitted to intimidate or influence any representative.

The notion of important lobbyists trying to influence legislators can have a negative effect on the clear thinking of the people's elected representatives. Let the lobbyists identify themselves and lobby the governed, not the instruments of their government.

The notion of lobbyists, however, is just an aside. If our representatives, paid well of course, ($174,000 per year as of 2009 not including expenses --- for each house seat knew that they could not receive additional compensation from lobbyists, bribers, or whatever you want to call them, ever, no how, no matter how they voted, they would not be as inclined to favor those for private interests against those for public interests.

Pay them well

Politicians live in elite neighborhoods. This is not good, but it would not be right to dictate the neighborhood in which your representative lives as long as it is within your district. Our representatives must be paid well for their service and they should believe that they are being paid well. Otherwise, their honesty may be compromised as they turn to the elite in order to receive more compensation.

They must be paid well during their terms and their terms must be short so that they do not become untouchable by mere mortals. The temptation of being for oneself while in office clearly must be minimized.

This is as we say, a representative democracy and our representatives cannot do well by the people if they represent themselves or those who are not of the people. It really is that simple. The primary point of this discussion is that we the people must reengage our government within the honorable laws (and we need to get rid of the laws not so honorable) that benefit all of the people.

Minimize the opportunity for corruption

Sending our newly elected into a quagmire of corruption and deceit and seeing who survives is not a good recipe for the future. Let's figure out how to get rid of the corruption and all the bad that comes with that. Calling the newly elected "the Honorable" and paying homage to her or him as a new governor of subjects is clearly not the right approach. It is unfortunately today's modus operandi, an operando that has long failed the people.

Thank-you's are most appropriate for good service. The notion of a required "hizzoner" that starts a period of aristocratic living from the first waltz of the Inaugural Ball, breeds just more separation from the people. In a democracy, the rich and the plebeians have the right to a voice in their government.

So, what do we do? Well, first of all we must realize that nothing is going to change for the better unless the people are very insistent. Corruption begins as the corrupt begin to believe in themselves and not the mission of helping their whole constituency. Rule # 1 for the people is to pay attention.

Unfortunately, as innocuous as it may seem, this notion of "The Honorable" and all that means, is ingrained deeply into the fabric of American political culture and etiquette. Until recently, however, one could also rely on the ethics and morals of the representatives as an additional inhibitor to corruption, and thus assuring proper action.

It seems that in the latter part of the 20th century the culture of "anything goes" has permeated American society and its morals and its ethics. Not all politicians are corrupt, but it is easy for our representatives to get sucked in to something that is much bigger than they themselves.

Therefore, one can no longer count on one's own ethics and one's own morals if elected to serve as a countervailing force against bad representation. Consequently, it is up to the people to create an environment, which is more personally rewarding for our representatives to do their jobs, than it would be to accept praise for merely being elected.

Political corruption is actually what we hope to prevent. When it was once safe to speak of religious values in this country without fear of reprisal or a lawsuit, there was an apparent social conscience with which to gauge all actions. Much of the writing of the founding fathers reflects a Christian bias for example.

The underlying Christian faith, which is based on love and honesty and goodness is not really a bad model upon which to form a government. I know of no Christian or Hindu or Jew who by ideology alone wants to kill me.

Ethics and morals

As our representatives get further removed from their original neighborhoods and become rich in one way or another because of their public service, this may help the representative, but it does not help the people. One teaching of the Christian church is the "eye of needle" analogy. Christianity holds that this is bad news for the rich, because it is easier for a camel to go through the eye of a needle than for a rich man to enter the kingdom of Heaven.

So, according to Christian teaching (the faith of the founding fathers), the tendency of a politician to work with the well-to-do and live in their neighborhoods while becoming rich makes them less likely to be worthy of Heaven. Less likely for Heaven means more likely for corruption and so, if honor is given in any form, perhaps it should be from the people to its representatives -- those representatives who stay in the regular neighborhoods and live humble lives. The representative would be honoring the people by doing so and would have more of an opportunity to avoid the needle test.

What might be the curing hypotheses using the scientific method that we pass to the next phase in the process (testing)? As my wife would say, "'What's the point?" Well, since you asked, this is exactly the point:

Representatives of the people at all levels of government are of the people and must therefore be for the people so that their laws can be recognized clearly as being by the people. When situations occur that exalt the representative regardless of their service or lack of service to the people, merely by their elected office, this is reprehensible, and the laws put forth under these circumstances should be viewed accordingly and scorned.

How can a pack of nothing but "Honorables," who have distanced and disconnected themselves from the ordinary people that elected them, represent us fairly in our government? The fact is that as a whole, today's representatives are not doing the people's business. They are doing their own business and the business of their elite sponsors. This problem is the very essence and the rationale of this book.

Thomas Jefferson had great disdain and mistrust for the propensity of man, once given the power to rule, to use that power for the good of the people rather than himself. He warned of what could happen when such people create issues for society that require more and more debt and ultimately more taxation, with the implication of poor representation. With historically high deficits and mounting national debt, we seemingly have not learned this lesson well:

> "We must not let our rulers load us with perpetual debt. We must make our election between economy and liberty or profusion and servitude. If we run into such debt, as that we must be taxed in our meat and in our drink, in our necessaries and our comforts, in our labors and our amusements, for our calling and our creeds...we [will] have no time to think, no means of calling our miss-managers to account but be glad to obtain subsistence by hiring ourselves to rivet their chains on the necks of our fellow-sufferers. And this is the tendency of all human governments. A departure from principle in one instance becomes a precedent till the bulk of society is reduced to be mere automatons of misery. And the foreshores of this frightful team is public debt. Taxation follows that, and in its train wretchedness and oppression."

Does it not seem in these words that Thomas Jefferson is looking at us from the grave, knowing his words have been unheeded and working for God now to make sure we get his message and we act accordingly?

Completed Hypotheses - Scientific Method

The solution to the "Honorables" is quite simple. Our elected representatives, while in Washington or in the state assemblies and even in the courtrooms and the lower legislatures, executive branch chambers, and councils should be treated with respect and should have amenities to compensate them well for their time away from home. However, they are not entitled to the title, "honorable" merely by taking the oath of office one time. The title "honorable" no longer can be an expected gift from the public to the representatives without them having earned the title. It is the legislators, executives, and justices themselves who should strip themselves of the title immediately and be done with it. It is nonsense and should be ceased immediately.

Additional Thoughts

Those once in office but no longer in office who still get a kick out of being called the "honorable" can receive a replacement title if it is that important to them, from the body from which they retired. Ex-presidents and ex-Governors and Ex-Mayors can request the title from an ad-hoc committee respectively made up of ex-Presidents, ex-Governors, and ex-Mayors. A suitable respectable title that does not imply honor can be created, such as "the public servant" or the "friend of the people," and this can be used in etiquette from henceforth rather than force a vote about honor for each public official above a certain level of office.

A different term for judges than "Your Honor " should be instituted and while in session, judges would thus be greeted as "Your Judgeship" while presiding officially in a courtroom. Since "judgeship accurately reflects the high respect needed for the position of judge, not the person behind the robes, it is a responsible compromise from the "honor" system.

In all other social events other than those purely political in nature and sponsored by politicians or friends of politicians, all of our duly elected servants should not be greeted as "the Honorable" or by their official title. In a democracy, if these people are of the people, and they are or should be, they should be addressed as all of the people are addressed. As an example, I do not want to be known as His Authorship.

If we think about it, we are all pretending about the elected being honorable anyway and that is just silly. It's actually pretty stupid besides. It's pure puffery at its best and in this day and age in which the constituency is questioning the loyalty of its representatives, considering ones-self as "the honorable," is not the side of the puff on which a representative should want to find himself.

The next phase of the scientific method of problem solving is as follows:

3. **Test the Hypothesis** - In this third phase of the scientific method, an experiment is performed to determine if the hypothesis solves the problem or not. Experiments are done to gather data. It is very important that good observations and records are made during an experiment.

Mary K. Mewborn, writing in the November 19, 1999 edition of *Washington Life Magazine,* in an article aptly titled "Too Many Honorables?" has done most of my work for me in testing the hypothesis. The solution as noted above is to not haphazardly bestow the title of "Honorable" - period. Ms. Mewborn notes the asininity involved in granting such a title in her first examples. Here are three priceless misuses of the title from Ms. Mewborn:

"A socialite in Wesley Heights thinks it adds personal distinction to her many listings on fundraising invitations."

"A former ambassador living at the Watergate uses it to remind others of his long-ago diplomatic posting to a small Caribbean nation."

"Appointees to even the most minor Presidential commissions are apt to believe it bestows instant social cachet- with invitations to A-list parties sure to follow."

She points out in this article that it is illegal to take the title "honorable," although she acknowledges that which cannot be gained legally can be gained by political process. In other words, the politicians can do what they want once they run the country -- and they do -- and they have -- and quite frankly that's why she and we are upset!

Test the reasonableness of no longer conferring the title honorable on our representatives by reading the following several paragraphs, again taken from Mary K. Mewborn's timeless article about "Too Many Honorables." Before the paragraphs, here is the URL of the article, available online for the surfing. It's a fun read.

http://www.washingtonlife.com/backissues/archives/99nov/honorables.htm

Whether it is the roster of the Board of Governors of the Smithsonian Institution or the benefit committee of a typical Washington charity gala, there are always a number of names preceded by "Honorable," instead of the usual Mr., Mrs., Miss or Ms. How this came about in a country whose Constitution expressly forbids the granting of titles amuses some and irritates others. At the very least its widespread usage raises some eyebrows.

Traditionally the British use the "Hon." (originally abbreviated from "The Right Honorable Magnificence of Nobles"), to identify certain family members of hereditary barons and earls, i.e., their daughters, younger sons and the younger sons' wives. In America, however, such inherited titles were rare among the early colonists, and after independence there was no king to grant new ones.

That did not mean this country developed along totally egalitarian lines. Even in a democracy it was only natural that ways had to be found to distinguish the elite from the hoi polloi, the rulers from the ruled. The conferment of titles, although prevented by the Constitution, was effectively achieved by political success.

Political primacy is now well-established in matters of protocol and etiquette and is, according to the U.S. Government, a matter of procedure and form. Consequently, it would be very improper indeed to refer to the "Hon. Bill Gates," even though he may have billions in the bank and pays his taxes, or to the "Hon. Cindy Crawford," although what man wouldn't hope to flatter her? Nobel Prizes and great humanitarian deeds won't make you Honorable either, though getting elected Mayor of Bladensburg, Md. definitely will.

By the rules of etiquette, you can become Honorable by getting elected to the White House or Congress, or by having the President nominate and the Senate confirm you to an ambassadorship or other political post (judge, commissioner, etc.). Once you are made an Honorable, you stay that way for life, regardless of what an independent counsel or district attorney may subsequently uncover about any untoward activities. "In Washington, as Betty Beale, longtime social columnist and observer of the Washington social scene, bluntly puts it, "The title `Honorable' has nothing to do either with honor or character."

The next phase of the scientific method of problem solving is as follows:

4. **Collect the Data** - Using the Scientific Method, this is the place in the process in which you record your observations, measurements, or information from experiment.

The collection of data in the scientific method can be represented by the copious research work that permitted Ms. Mewborn to uncover the fact that the title "honorable" is not and cannot be a conferred title and therefore it is a title that is improperly used to refer to the people's representatives merely because of their representation. The raw data from her research is not here for us to examine but there is enough in her article to suffice as data well collected.

Moreover, you and I have observed the notion of the "Honorables" in our daily lives and we have also seen the impact of such pomposity in the behavior of our elected officials. If you have looked at the same news accounts as I way back in 2009 and 2010 with the Obama presidency and long before, it is clear that our representatives have become so honorable that there is now so much honor, there is no longer any room for shame. There is a lot of collected data in our observations and those of the media.

In the Federal Government, it is clear that Senators are further away from the people than members of the House of Representatives. They behave as Lords from old England and have a major disconnect with the people. Even when they commit a crime, they believe they are better than the "represented."

Among just about every highlight reel from the five to ten years ago, is the story of a US senator who said he would resign in the midst of scandal surrounding his arrest in a police sting targeting lewd behavior in a men's public restroom. However, realizing he was a senator after admitting guilt, he then flip flopped believing his own admission of guilt was not enough to prove that he was guilty. Pomposity with a grand title of "yeronner," makes it even worse.

Remember Senator Larry Craig, 62 at the time, who had been arrested in June 2007 but then pleaded guilty in August to a lesser charge - disorderly conduct. He apparently paid the $500 fine, and was given a 10-day suspended sentences and a year's probation. But, he was only kidding...

Another class act is Democratic Congressman William "the Freezer" Jefferson of Louisiana. Jefferson has been dubbed the "Freezer" though he has no major football skills but until recently he had been able to avoid the rush.

In the first edition of this book, I was able to say that he had not been sacked yet, but his sack was found in his freezer with $90,000 of cold, in fact, frozen cash. He's in jail now. His constituents more than likely gave him the cash from a number of lemonade sales they undertook to help him with his future defense if he were ever to need cash. OK, I lie but the story is pretty close.

The Congressman faced 16 charges of being a thief, more than 2 years after the FBI found the cash in his freezer. He was convicted on 11 of the counts. That does not mean he was not guilty on the others. He was guilty of taking a bribe from a foreign official and the $90,000 was left from the marked $100,000 that he received (from an FBI Informant). After all, $100,000 is a lot to spend. Fearing he would take off to a remote island, Jefferson was remanded before sentencing. How's that for honor?

As a result of these two and others of less recent vintage such as Republican Duke Cunningham, Republican Bob Ney and Democrat Jim Traficant and probably hundreds more like them, it has become easy to presume guilt. Of course, I don't have to tell you about Michigan's John Conyers or Minnesota's Al Franken—both fine men surely. They are stepping down because they are "honorable."

As noted previously, "How can you tell if a politician is lying? He's moving his lips." That says it all, but it helps to repeat it to remember it.

Dr. Gerhard Falk, writing an article in blog form on http://jbuff.com/c012705.htm performed his research and collected data in order to shed some light on the subject of respect for politicians. Whether you agree with all of what he said or not, Falk certainly caught the spirit of the great disdain with which our leaders were held in 2008 and not much has changed since.

Mewborn and Falk and many others with whom we would probably agree, note that the "Honorables" have created an ironically dishonorable circumstance, some by their conduct outside of office and some by their poor representation. The moniker of "honorable" being used to describe those looked upon as of questionable repute does not help matters. Dr. Falk adds his own few words about the Honorables to the mix as he discusses the vile of politicians in his blog:

> Politicians of all parties are evidently convinced that the whole world revolves only around them. They do not want to meet the voters, i.e. the ordinary taxpayers, for fear that they may be asked what they do all day and what happed to our money. They call themselves "the honorable" this and that...
> ...
>
> Politicians love to aggrandize themselves. Bill Clinton spent $42 million on his second inauguration and George W. Bush spent $40 million more. These expensive theatrics are obscene and have no place in our democracy. Read the life of George Washington. He was sworn in for a second time as President of the United States on March 4, 1793. His speech was only 134 words and he then walked home alone. No parade. No speeches. No dances. No gross exhibition of ego.

Falk had not met Barack Obama, the first combination Sultan. King, and President of the US. Because of the triple duty, Obama was forced to spend upwards of $170 million for his inauguration. Was it inflation or excessive self-love?

For the pure scientist who is reading this, please forgive my poetic license regarding the scientific method and the idea of data collection to back up the hypotheses. Once all the data for this phase would be collected, there would be plenty to affirm the validity of the hypothesis and the analysis.

The next phase of the scientific method of problem solving is as follows:

5. **Analyze the Data** - This part of the Scientific Method asks the question: "Just what does all that data indicate about answering the problem you are solving?"

The problem of self-aggrandizement and the notion of self-importance are well documented and well observed even without deploying the scientific method. Will the inability to use the title "Honorable" actually solve the problem of (1) inappropriate claiming of title and (2) the resultant lack of true representation of the people for the people by the representatives of the people?

The scientific method helps us here even though we cannot observe the results of the blocking of the use of the title since there is no real data and no true table upon which to experiment. However, since this problem limited itself to part 1 of 2 in the prior paragraph, the answer is logically clear that if the title "honorable" can no longer be used in a whimsical manner by any politician at any time, then the problem statement is solved by the hypothesis. Thus, we can stage the analysis to draw such conclusions in Step 6.

However, there is no real set of data that can be collected (Step 4) that would tell us that our representatives would actually change their behavior and be more prone to represent the people rather than themselves or special interests. We would hope so but there are no assurances. Most reasonable, prudent people would believe that it would contribute to a better situation, but it probably would not be enough.

The next phase of the scientific method of problem solving is as follows:

6. **Draw Conclusions** - After examining the data from the experiment, at this point in the six-point Scientific Method process, conclusions can be drawn. In its simplest form, the conclusion will be "yes" the hypothesis is correct, or "no" the hypothesis is not correct.

The solution as noted previously is simple to the problem of the "Honorables." If they no longer are bestowed the title merely by gaining an office or an appointment, the problem of "too many Honorables" and not enough honor is on its way to a successful ending.

Once politicians can no longer hijack the title, "Honorable," their egos will no longer be instantly stroked, and the people will have eliminated one major source of puffery for our duly elected representatives.

Let honor be reserved for honorable deeds and not because politicians may be offended if there is not an aura of puff surrounding their entrance onto the scene. So, we can say **Yes** to this conclusion and I would suggest that we should say it loudly.

-- End of Scientific Method ---

But is puffery really the problem?

Heavens no! But, puffery is a big problem since it is the arrogant, puffed-up politician who is more likely to choose to disrespect the will of the people and go on his way to legislate for the good of himself or directly for special interests. Politicians go out of their way to bring wonderful legislative gifts to the privileged class and the special interests. The current "Honorables" have a hard time saying "No" to friends in high places. Thank you, Garth Brooks.

I received a number of emails this year from cohorts who, like you are interested in this U.S. government succeeding. Most, like you and I find major fault with such a representation process that puts so many buffoons in office. We all know intuitively that the notion of humor is the quality that appeals to a sense of the ludicrous or absurdly incongruous. For those schooled in high school geometry, it's like when CPCT is not equal and cannot be equal.

When things do not add up and nobody is hurt, at least at the time of the adding, it sure can be funny and it can induce a big belly laugh. The puffery that comes with political office and the buffoonery of many of the "Honorables," is what I will attribute to this email that I received from one of my associates. I have no idea of the original source of this email but it sure captures what I have been trying to say about the perception of the character of our elected officials.

Subject: Haircut

One day a florist goes to a barber for a haircut. After the cut he asked about his bill and the barber replies, "I cannot accept money from you. I'm doing community service this week." The florist was pleased and left the shop. When the barber goes to open his shop the next morning there is a 'thank you' card and a dozen roses waiting for him at his door.

Later, a cop comes in for a haircut, and when he tries to pay his bill, the barber again replies, "I cannot accept money from you. I'm doing community service this week." The cop is happy and leaves the shop. The next morning when the barber goes to open up there is a 'thank you' card and a dozen donuts waiting for him at his door.

Later that day, a college professor comes in for a haircut, and when he tries to pay his bill, the barber again replies, "I cannot accept money from you. I'm doing community service this week." The professor is very happy and leaves the shop. The next morning when the barber opens his shop, there is a 'thank you' card and a dozen different books, such as "How to Improve Your Business" and Becoming More Successful."

"Then, a Congressman comes in for a haircut, and when he goes to pay his bill the barber again replies, "I cannot accept money from you. I'm doing community service this week." The Congressman is very happy and leaves the shop. The next morning when the barber goes to open up, there are a dozen Congressmen lined up waiting for a free haircut.

And that, my friends, illustrates the fundamental difference between the citizens of our country and the members of our Congress.

This little email joke may not say it all but it sure says a lot about the breakdown in real respect that the people have for the representatives of the people. As you will see in the other chapters of this book, there are lots of real reasons for this feeling and it is not just a matter of puff.

Chapter Summary

In this chapter we used the scientific method to determine whether there was a real problem with all of the fluff and puff that is associated with our political class. The use of the word "Honorable" was the point that was debated in this chapter. Should our elected representatives be entitled to the title "Honorable" merely by being elected. Using the Scientific Method, we concluded that the answer is no and that it hurts our democratic system of representative egalitarian government to suggest that all men are not equal.

Chapter 8 A Civics Lesson: Constitutional Democracy

The US is a Constitutional Republic

This chapter introduces the notion of the importance of representative government to the citizens of the United States and it also introduces the notion of taxation without representation as our elected leaders fail to accomplish their duties. In this Civics Lesson, we examine the form of our representative democracy and we explore other forms and variations that make the US form of government about as good as it can get.

These brief civics lessons are presented in this book to give the reader the opportunity to understand the basic tenets of the US representative constitutional democracy. For a deeper appreciation of the notion of the US government and its underlying political principles, there is an excellent free course available on the Internet and I encourage you to visit the Cyberland University of North America at the following URL:

http://www.proconservative.net/CUNAPolSci201HOutline.shtml

Dr. Almon Leroy Way, Jr. University President & Professor of Political Science in his free Internet course titled Political Science 201H - The American Political System: Politics & Government in the USA captures the details of politics and government in America. It is an excellent reference for just about any facet of American Government and Politics that you would like to examine. My hat is off to Dr. Way for a wonderful work and a thank you for sharing it with us all. Below, you will find the course description taken from the Web Site:

COURSE DESCRIPTION:
A free, self-study, non-credit course in American Government and Politics designed to benefit (1) the general reader interested in politics, government, law, and public affairs, (2) the advanced high-school student enrolled in an American Government, Advanced Civics, Modern Problems, Problems of Democracy, or Political Science course, and (3) the university or college student enrolled in or planning to enroll in a Political Science or International Relations course or in a History, Geography, Sociology, Economics, or Business course with substantial political content.

Constitutional democracy & other political regimes

The United States of America has been formed as a "*constitutional democracy*." Democracy can be defined as government by the people or by their elected representatives. A "direct democracy" or as it is sometimes called, a "pure democracy" is a system in which all the people of a country or entity, who choose to participate do so directly without elected or appointed representatives. The latter is referred to as a representative democracy.

Attributes of a direct democracy are included in the notions of Initiation (opportunity to propose legislation), Referendum (opportunity to offer ballot resolutions in elections) on a ballot, and Recall (the ability to vote to have representatives come back home so that a better representative can be chosen from the people. Unfortunately, these attributes are not included in the federal government of the United States, but they are included in a number of state constitutions.

The specific makeup of a direct democracy may take on different capabilities depending on the will of the people. Depending on how the system is structured, the members of this assembly might pass executive orders, create laws, elect and dismiss leaders and conduct trials. When elected officials conduct the people's business in a direct democracy, they are considered executive agents or direct representatives and thus are bound to the will of the people.

Today's US representatives believe they are charged like the Carnac the Magnificent, played by Johnny Carson to divine the will of the people, rather than listen to the people, and do whatever they choose based upon their divining. A Direct Democracy would force the stand-ins for the people to vote in ways the people have dictated.

Considering that many citizens of the US are upset with our leaders because of little accountability, the notion of leaders being tied to the will of the people at first seems to have substantial merit.

With over 300,000,000 and counting as the population of the US, one can also see how it may be unwieldy for such a system to be fully direct in practice regardless of how attractive it is in theory. Thus, for a direct democracy to work, intermediary public groups are needed.

Theoretically, these groups can be the state legislators but, this too has issues in that the notion of "Honorables" and poor representation of the people's interests is also a major ailment of state governments.

Nonetheless, the vehicles that are used in a direct democracy - namely, Initiative, Referendum, and Recall all have merit and need to be included soon as amendments to our constitution for our Federal Government.

When the representatives choose not to do the will of the people, a form of government that inhibits actions directly by the people gets in the way of being able to handle the situation. There is always the wonderful idea that when they are not doing their jobs, we can throw the bums out, by not reelecting them, and we should.

But with the entanglements that our elected find themselves with the ruling class, waiting two to six years to throw them out can be "taxing" and it makes the system less effective and less responsive than employing some direct democracy notions within our constitutional democracy. How many of us would like the opportunity to have e legitimate means to simply throw these liars and cheats out of office.

You see, it is a constitutional democracy that governs the US using the representative democracy form of government. And thus, the term *constitutional* democracy implies a number of structural points as follows:

- The basic principles upon which the society of the United States of America operates
- The institutional forms and processes of the U.S. government
- The distribution of political authority among the major offices and institutions of the government
- The resulting power relationships among these government offices and institutions.

The notion of constitutionalism strengthens democracy as it defines the underlying principles in which the democratic structure is to operate. The founders trusted nobody, but their pens and their pens wrote the Constitution and all prior documents making the Constitutional Republic of the USA a reality.

It clearly differs from other forms of government not chosen by our founding fathers such as dictatorships and oligarchies -- though many scholars today suggest that the US in practice, with the tacit acceptance of the political class and the governed, is becoming more of an oligarchy in which the few rule the many. That's why I wrote this book. We have to put an end to that notion.

This was clearly not the intention of the founding fathers in developing the outline for constitutional democracy that has worked so well for so long. Pay attention to what the founders intended, please.

Now that we have defined the notion of a democracy, what then makes a constitutional democracy that much different?

A constitutional democracy can be described accurately as a system of government in which the power of government is defined and thus limited, and it is distributed in a body of fundamental written law called "the Constitution." Additionally, the electorate (that's us - the people -- a.k.a. the general voting populace within our political society) is given the effective means of controlling the elected representatives in the government and holding them accountable for their decisions and actions while in public office. Does that not sound idealistically simple in theory?

A constitutional democracy thus has two essential ingredients, (1) a *constitutional* ingredient and (2) a *democratic* ingredient. Let's examine these ingredients:

The ***constitutional*** ingredient of a constitutional democracy is the "*constitutional government.*" As noted above, this means that the founding fathers wrote a constitution so that the elected representatives of this nation could not just go ahead and do whatever they pleased with no constraints. The founders did not want them doing whatever they wanted with complete disregard to the most basic law of this country - its Constitution.

The *democratic* ingredient of a constitutional democracy is *representative democracy* and, as noted previously, it has to do with who holds and thus has the right to exercise authority on behalf of the governed. It also describes how such authority is acquired and retained (elections, impeachments etc.).

Additionally, it prescribes that the representatives of the people are accountable to the people, and through elections, the people can change the face of the government by changing the face of its representatives. -- i.e. throwing the bums out...

A *constitution* as noted above is a very important document in that it provides the opportunity to protect liberty and freedom beyond the lives of the founders of the government. For the United States of America, its Constitution is the *supreme* law of land. Thus, it is of higher importance and takes precedence over all other laws of society.

In fact, all other laws, to be valid and enforceable, must be written in accordance with the superior law of the Constitution. Thus, in recent years, a number of cases, in which laws were passed about matters of great importance such as abortion, have been appealed to the Supreme Court of the U.S., the court of last resort which determines whether laws pass the constitutional sniff test.

When the laws do not pass the test or when the political makeup of the court sees things in a different light, laws created by the states and by the federal legislature are either upheld or not upheld. Thus, they can or cannot be enforced.

On April 16, 2007, for example, the Supreme Court chose to uphold a law that banned a type of late-term abortion, a ruling that many believe portends enormous social, legal and political implications regarding this very divisive issue.

Considering that the nine members of the court itself were sharply divided (5-4) could prove historic. Political analysts suggested at the time that it sent a possible signal of the court's willingness, under Chief Justice John Roberts, to someday revisit the right to abortion which heretofore had been guaranteed in the 1973 Roe v. Wade case. Let's see over time what happens in this one case.

No branch of government is exempt from following the Constitution. In the U.S., every law enacted by a legislature and every decision or action of an executive office or agency must pass the constitutional test. Not all laws that may be unconstitutional by definition if well examined, however, are challenged in court.

For a law to be reversed it must be appealed and can be appealed as many times as needed until it may reach the Supreme Court of the United States. If the governmental decision or law or action in question is found by the courts to be contrary to the Constitution, the court system will uphold the Constitution and set aside the unconstitutional decision or action of the legislature or of the executive branches. At least that is the sworn duty of the courts.

Each state in the Union of States has its own constitution thus giving the 50 states a notion of semi-autonomy (partly self-governing). These states comprise the federal union. The US Constitution guides the operation of the national government, and establishes its formal power relationships between the national government and the 50 semiautonomous states as well as the formal power relationships among the principal organs, or institutions, of the national government.

None of us would want this power left to folklore or to memory alone as it is far too important. Thus, it is written in the body of text known as the Constitution.

The U.S. Constitution is in fact, a single document consisting of the seven original articles drafted by the Federal Constitutional Convention of 1787, which were eventually ratified by the 13 original colonies (states). Besides these original notions, there are 27 amendments that have been added to the Constitution during the 200+ years that have elapsed since ratification and adoption of the Constitution. The first ten of these amendments are known collectively as The Bill of Rights.

The US *constitutional system* consists of the power relationships among the principal branches of government resulting from the constitutional division and distribution of political authority among them by the Constitution itself. It defines the roles in the governing process played by each of the principal governmental institutions defined within the Constitution.

This is very important for Americans in that the Constitution provides the following attributes of government on our behalf:

- Divides and distributes the authority of government between the central government over the whole nation and the governments of the member-states of the federal union
- Assigns certain governmental powers to the states, while denying them certain other powers
- Assigns certain powers to the national government and expressly prohibits it from exercising certain other powers,
- Assigns the powers delegated to the national government to the principal entities of that government (the U.S. House of Representatives, the U.S. Senate, the President of the U.S.A., and the U.S. Courts). This is a key ingredient and serves the need for major checks and balances of power and it assures that the government does not run away from the people to begin to govern independently. Each entity has its own power, a strong incentive, and a legal right to oppose, block, check, and restrain the other entities of government if they get off track.
- Prescribes certain limitations on both the central government and the states by guaranteeing *civil liberties*, i.e., the basic rights and liberties of the individual citizen.

The U.S. Government has been set up to be constitutional in character. However, it does not necessarily follow that all branches of government will adhere to this precept and by neglect or by the political process, facets of the constitutionality of the government can be overridden in fact if not in deed. The US government must comply with two fundamental legal requirements to remain legitimate

- The government must operate in accordance with the provisions of the Constitution
- The government must not exceed the authority granted to it by the Constitution.

As much as we like our political representatives, we do not want them taking more power than we are willing to give them. When you read the Constitution, it is clear how insightful the founding fathers were as they built the essential features of constitutionalism into the framework of the US government. The government's compliance with these two basic legal requirements are essential to its legitimacy.

So, if we were to summarize the central purpose of constitutionalism, we would show that it is to protect ourselves from our too-far-reaching neighbors who become politicians to promote their own welfare. The notion of limiting governmental power as dictated in the Constitution checks and restraints on the persons who hold public office and exercise political authority is at the top of those precepts necessary. And it is up to us—you and I—as a wary and watchful society that this government does not get out of control -- and hopefully this book will help us all in this regard.

Therefore, we cannot watch as our democracy is shattered, and the rule of law provided by our Constitution is abrogated or abridged for political expediency. The rule of law strongly implies that there are limits to political authority, that there are limits to the power of any governing elite to rule society. The people own the government - not vice versa. All the entities of government-- the legislative and executive branches, and the administrative agencies under control of the President, and even the courts of law--are all required to observe and operate according to the law of the land—The Constitution.

Who is important in America?

The protection of individual rights and liberties is a major tenet of the rule of law. The people permit the laws to be enacted and enforced and the law guarantees each individual citizen certain rights and liberties and protects them from arbitrary interference or deprivation by government officeholders.

The Constitution and the rule of law are vital to preventing a runaway government like we find in many other parts of the world, such as Russia, Cuba, and Venezuela.

The government cannot legally deprive a person of life, liberty, or property without due process of law. That is, the government, in taking punitive action against a person, is required to act in strict accordance with legally established procedures.

The government caretakers (our elected officials) cannot, without violating the law, arbitrarily execute or imprison an individual or confiscate his property, disregarding the established rules of procedure.

It does not matter whether the special interests would applaud such behavior, the rule of law is not intended to benefit the special interests and the elite ruling class. It is for the people.

What if the Founding Fathers formed a different kind of government?

The founding fathers could have made George Washington the King of America instead of our first President. The people loved Washington and more than likely would have accepted him as king. However, the founders had already had enough of King George III and another King George would not have set well with them.

Thomas Jefferson made his point with just these few words right on point: "An elective despotism was not the government we fought for." Jefferson and the founding fathers could have given George Washington dictatorial powers if they chose, but what if George decided things about America that were good for George and not good for Americans?

What would be their recourse under the "new" law? None -- nada, zilch, squat... and thus this was not a good system to choose and it was not chosen. If you'll pardon me for saying it, in a dictatorship, they'd have had to "let George do it."

The founders could have formed a constitutional Oligarchy instead of a democracy. This basically is a system in which there is no representation and the few rule the many under the rules of a Constitution, written by the few.

The good news in this approach is that there is typically a body of law - the constitution. The bad news is that laws can be created or taxes imposed that can negatively affect the people with no recourse but to accept.

Thank the founders for our America

Considering that the major squabble with England was about taxation without representation, it would have been unlikely for the founding fathers to fight a revolution that would not provide for individual rights and liberties through a representative form of government.

The US Constitution in the 1780's was written to assure these benefits and to keep the politicians from taking the country in a direction contrary to the will of the people, which they seem to have done over the last 50 years or more, anyway.

If it were not that political power, as in the notion that the political class is comprised of politicians, with the assent or tacit acceptance of all three branches, can in fact be wielded against the population, the issues of government today might be as minimal as in the late 18th century after independence was gained. But today's politicians think they own the people.

In other words, "grabby" politicians separate themselves from the people, so they can serve themselves and other masters. Our founders did not need a remedy for lobbyists or real term limitations. Those issues were non-existent.

Now, the voters of our time are way too busy to pay attention and thus, they are easily duped by the politicos into electing the same bums each time their terms are up. What a shame. Thankfully many Americans continue to think for themselves.

For its part, even the Supreme Court has its political motivations and sometimes its actions are questionable. Clearly there are those who believe that George Bush would have had a second term, if it were not for Sandra Day O'Connor and the other four Justices of the US Supreme Court.

And, a new notion of eminent domain recently was determined by the court that permits political agents to confiscate your land and property for the good of someone else. Whoever did this must be replaced.

Many, and I include myself among them, believe this latter idea goes so far beyond the intentions of those who drafted the US constitution that it is actually humorous - but in a sick way. It needs to be overturned.

So, the conclusion may be that our Constitutional Democracy. Aka, our Republic, is pretty good, but it is far from perfect, mostly because it is administered and interpreted by human beings who have natural bias. Let's end the lesson now!

Sources

http://www.washingtonlife.com/backissues/archives/99nov/honorables.htm

http://www.proconservative.net/CUNAPolSci201HOutline.shtml

Chapter 9: Taxes, Taxes, and More Taxes

Everything costs something

You make it. They take it! Most of our representatives, who are good at their trade (politicians), never met a tax they didn't like. Nobody can deny that there is none better at bringing in the big ones than the current president of the US. He took the money and nobody even knew it came from them. Yup! It came from you. The many ingenious types of taxes we find throughout the U. S. prove that a motivated politician is as clever at least as the U.S. Chief Executive and surely as prolific as a con man in figuring out how to remove dollars from your wallet and place them in the government treasury.

After all, only with lots of tax revenue can politicians become folk heroes by taking some of this plunder and "creating jobs" or giving grants to other government bodies or corporations to strengthen their reelection opportunities. They thrive on income redistribution. Yours becomes theirs. They have just two goals:

1. Continuance in office (reelection)
2. Opportunity for a better office

In the first year of Obama, the government seemed not to care where he big payoffs would have to come from. But, now, of course we know what is coming. No matter what they appear to be working on, taking your money is their prime mission in life. Keep this in mind: Politicians serving as our representatives will not be denied their share of your income. It enables them to achieve their two major goals.

Of course, there are good, God-fearing people serving as representatives and they are not all bad when they get elected. Some stay good, but it sure seems that today they are in the minority. When the clock says there is just enough time left to get elected, that's where they focus their energies. Whether it serves us or not, reelection and the chance of a higher office trumps anything the represented may have had on their minds.

Government's share of your income is increasing

According to The Tax Foundation, a nonprofit group whose mission it is to keep taxes to an absolute minimum, in 2007 Americans worked longer to pay for government (120 days) than they did for food, clothing and housing combined (105 days). Since 1986 taxes have cost more than these basic necessities. In fact, Americans have to work longer to afford federal taxes alone (79 days) than they do to afford housing (62 days). And, of course, that's not even counting state and local taxes! But, we are about to count them, literally, because they count big time.

US Citizens are sometimes asked to pay up -- to three or four and perhaps more intertwined levels of government. For example, United States taxation most certainly includes local government. Local Government on the other hand, refers to one or more of municipal, township, district and county governments. It also includes regional entities such as school and utility, and transit districts. Oh, did we mention the state and federal government? Having a closed wallet or purse in these modern times is tantamount to teasing the government. And when they find out... well...

We'll put off our discussion of Federal taxes for just a bit since most taxpayers already feel its sting and understand it in many ways. Besides, the Federal Government and its "honorable representatives" do not have to be as ingenious to bilk their constituencies out of the fruits of their labor. By the way, that "constituencies" word, that means us...

So, is there anything we can do about it? Oh, yeah there is but nothing happens overnight. The first step is being aware. The second step is making sure you read the rest of the book.

Heading off to Peoria

Some, especially retirees and the plain old rich, are so fed up with the state and local tax situation that they admit that they up and go "shopping" periodically for a new state or locale in which to live. Their motivation is nothing more than to pay less taxes. Most of us may go to the mall for a break while these of us head for the Interstate Highway System, only to find that the Federal Government has permitted the states to make them toll roads. So, on the trip to financial freedom, their wallets must open to pay the "road use tax."

Maybe Peoria is not the right place and maybe it is. The facts are that in 2010, just seven of the 50 states have no state income tax. Yes, we'll tell you who they are -- Alaska, Florida, Nevada, South Dakota, Texas, Washington and Wyoming. Hey, there are two others, New Hampshire and Tennessee, who tax only dividend and interest income. Such a deal.

Una fortuna, for most of us, the choice of where we are going to live the rest of our lives is often decided when we buy a home in our favorite city and we live in "our town" for enough years to make it home if it wasn't always home. And many of us, still live in our home towns. While this get-up-and-go notion may be fine for some, the burden of taxation is so imposing that there are others who don't care what the cost may be to get out, they are highly motivated to keep their income or their retirement from the grasp of greedy politicians, who are always ready to grab it. Those who do not feel a major loyalty to a particular state, simply take off and find states where the tax burden is lighter -- or so it seems at least.

If you are inclined to travel to keep more of your wealth, it pays to examine the tax burden you'll face when you arrive in your new state. State taxes are increasingly important to everyone, but retirees especially have cause for concern since their income in many cases is fixed. In a land of rising, punitive taxes, the future actually looks dimmer and dimmer. While you sleep, in addition to a number of other self-serving plans, your "noble" representatives are plotting to find new ways to get your last dollar. If they can do it with chicaneries, without your being aware, their thrill of victory is even sweeter for them -- but for you the bitterness endures.

The retiree is a special case since their incomes are fixed and whimsical taxes can play a big part in how much is left when the day is done. Many planning to retire and ready to use the presence or absence of a state income tax as a litmus test for a good retirement destination. This may be a very serious mistake since higher property taxes and sales taxes and nuisance taxes such as in the lists below can more than offset the lack of a state income tax. The point, of course is be careful if your car is warming up outside.

Though it is a definite plus for a state to not have an income tax-- especially if the first letters of your states name is as follows:

C-A-L-I-F-O-R-N-I-A: there are other reasons to stay away from certain states, especially if your state's name is C-A-L-I-F-O-R-N-I-A. At 10.3% for the highest bracket, this tax is punitive. New York State and NY City together are about 10.3%. So, the left and right coasts are pretty tough on the wallet. The highest state income tax, however is neither of these. The price to play in balmy and beautiful Hawaii is 11% max rate. These state taxes, of course are on top of the Federal Income Tax and the Payroll Tax (FICA and Medicare). It's a big load to carry.

If you escape high state income taxes, you still must be careful on your journey to low taxes. It doesn't necessarily ensure a low total tax burden. When you see this exhaustive but still incomplete list of tax titles, it will remind you that states raise revenue in many ways including sales and property taxes for sure but also with penalizing excise taxes, license taxes, intangible taxes, estate taxes and inheritance taxes. Moreover, you can bet there would be taxes on taxes (the infamous taxtax) if your hometown or state rep could get away with it.

Depending on where you live, you may end up paying all of them or if you are lucky, just a few. If you are planning to take up your cot and move out of town, the message is that you better be right.

We pay Uncle Sam the same no matter where we live, but property, gasoline, tobacco, sales and state income taxes are all over the map in the fifty states and again, they are not inconsequential. What should you look for if you hope to better yourself by moving or what should you look for so that you don't get snookered by politicians in your home state by staying the course? Let's start by looking at a number of the known ways that politicians obtain more revenue. (And, of course more revenue means you pay more taxes) What are some of the major types of taxes that state and local politicians have come up with since the Founding Fathers enjoyed the Atlantic Sea Salt in the tea of Boston in 1773?

You might be surprised but then again, you might not be. Take a look at these lists. This will get you agitated so be careful that you don't read more than 10 of these twisted con artist tricks at a time. Whether it agitates you or not, hold on to your purses and wallets while you check out the following income redistribution schemes that we can credit only to our "trusty" representatives:

Common state taxes

- Capitation, a fixed tax charged per person
- Cigarette Tax
- Fuel Tax
- Inheritance and Estate Taxes
- Personal Income Tax
- Property Tax
- Retirement Income Taxes
- Retired Military Pay
- State Income Tax
- State Sales Tax
- State Unemployment Tax

Less common state taxes

Though less common, these potentially substantive taxes, depending on your lifestyle, include the following:

- Alcoholic Beverage tax
- Alternative Minimum Tax
- Air Emissions Fee
- Auto Rental Tax

- Casino Gambling Taxes
- Charity Gaming Tax
- Consumers' Compensating Use Tax
- Contamination Tax
- Contractor Registration Fee/Tax
- Controlled Substance Tax
- Corporate Income Tax
- Corporation Registration Fee
- Deed Tax
- Dry Cleaner Fee/Tax
- Drug Stamp Tax
- <u>Drug Tax Stamps</u>
- Environmental Protection Charge
- Estate and Trust Tax
- Financial Institutions tax
- Franchise Tax
- Fur Clothing Tax
- Gross Receipts Tax
- Household Hazardous Materials Fee
- Household Hazardous Waste Fee
- Hotel / Innkeeper Tax
- Insurance Tax
- Jock Tax
- Lawful Gambling Tax
- Landfill fees
- Luxury Tax
- Mineral Tax
- Mobile Home Tax
- Motor Vehicle Use Tax
- Mortgage Registry Tax
- Ocean Marine Profit Tax
- Oil Inspection Fees/Taxes
- Other Tobacco Taxes
- Parimutual Tax
- Personal Property tax
- Real Estate Transfer Tax
- Riverboat Admissions tax
- Riverboat Wagering tax
- Sin Tax
- Soda Tax

Chapter 9 Taxes, Taxes, & More Taxes 87

- Special Fuel Tax
- Sports Bookmaking Tax
- Underground Storage Fuel Tax
- Unemployment Taxes
- Use Tax
- Water quality tax
- Wind Energy Production Tax
- Use Tax for individuals
- Utility Receipts Tax
- 911 Special tax

Local taxes

- Amusement Tax
- Building Permit Tax
- Businesses License Tax (*many types of businesses*)
- Cities & Municipalities Tax
- Development Income Tax
- Emergency & Municipal Services Tax (*Once called the Occupational Privilege Tax*)
- Earned Income Tax
- Health Permit Tax
- Jock Tax
- Mechanical Devices Tax
- Mercantile Tax
- Per Capita Tax
- Personal Property Tax
- Occupation Tax
- Parking Tax
- Parking Ticket Tax
- Real Property Tax
    County
    City
- Realty Transfer Tax
- Restaurant License Tax
- School District Taxes
    School Districts
- Taverns License Tax

Federal taxes

- Alternative Minimum Tax
- Bulk Alcohol Taxes
- Beer Taxes
- Liquor Tax
- Cigarette Tax
- Corporate Income Tax
- Currency Transaction Tax
- Estimated Tax
- Excess Profits Tax
- Federal Income Tax
- Federal Unemployment Tax
- Franchise Tax
- Fuel Tax
- Gift Taxes
- Highway Tax
- Internet Tax (When they think it's safe)
- Medicare Tax (FICA)
- Personal Income Tax
- Social Security Tax (FICA)
- Tariff (borders)
- Telephone Tax
- Tobacco Tax
- Wine Tax
- Etc. (I am getting tired)
- Yes there are more in each list

Recent taxes related just to Obamacare

- $123 Billion: Surtax on Investment Income – Capital Gains
- $86 Billion: Hike in Medicare Payroll Tax
- $65 Billion: Individual Mandate Excise Tax and Employer Mandate Tax
- $60.1 Billion: Tax on Health Insurers
- $32 Billion: Excise Tax on Comprehensive Health Insurance Plans
- $23.6 Billion: "Black liquor" tax hike

- $22.2 Billion: Tax on Innovator Drug Companies
- $20 Billion: Tax on Medical Device Manufacturers
- $15.2 Billion: High Medical Bills Tax
- $13.2 Billion: Flexible Spending Account Cap – aka "Special Needs Kids Tax"
- $5 Billion: Medicine Cabinet Tax
- $4.5 Billion: Elimination of tax deduction for employer-provided retirement Rx drug coverage i
- $4.5 Billion: Codification of the "economic substance doctrine"
- $2.7 Billion: Tax on Indoor Tanning Services
- $1.4 Billion: HSA Withdrawal Tax Hike
- $0.6 Billion: $500,000 Annual Executive Compensation Limit for Health Insurance Executives
- $0.4 Billion:
- $ Negligible: Excise Tax on Charitable Hospitals
- $ Negligible: Employer Reporting of Insurance on W-2

Send in what you want?

If I tried to tell you how the Federal Government was ripping you off on a system of income taxes that encourage cheating and assuming you are honest, you would be upset. I won't say that. But, one thing seems for certain, the Federal Government depends on the majority of its citizens to be honest and that is how they collect their tolls. What would be the alternative? Well, no politician on record has yet suggested that we just let it up to the people how much they choose to send in as their fair share just because they are honest.

The 2009 soda, drink, juice & milk tax

Just when you thought you were safe from more stupid taxes because they got them all covered, our Federal lawmakers figured out another one. This one is a tax on soda, drinks, juice, and even flavored milk. Obviously, the makers of all these items as well as consumers have lined up against this tax and because President Obama did not get his healthcare bill passed in the summer (passed in March 2010), the US may have escaped this tax for now. But, now that the tax man has discovered it, watch your juice budget.

While the tax man discovers more and more ways to tax the public, the public does fight back—especially on the 2009 Soda Tax. A review shows that 21 companies and organizations reported that they lobbied specifically on the proposed tax on sugar-sweetened beverages — which among other things would include sodas, juice drinks and chocolate milk.

I know you think it is already too ridiculous but putting a ridiculous tax to fund a ridiculous healthcare package so that ridiculous behaviourists can cause Americans to behave the way they would like is simply ridiculous, but true, nonetheless.

Yes, however, this tax on sugar-sweetened beverages, including flavoured milk, was in the initial list of revenue options released on May 18, 2009 by senators Max Baucus and Charles Grassley, chairman and ranking republican, respectively, on the Senate Finance Committee.

While they did not specifically give a tax rate, the speculators have looked at various options and costs. A tax of 3¢ per 12 fl. oz. for example could raise as much as $50 billion over 10 years to fund an overhaul of the nation's healthcare system, according to a congressional estimate. The Milk people who try everything to get kids to drink milk in any from rather than junk are outraged as one would expect. You may be able to slow the tax man, but sooner or later, the tax man cometh.

Chapter Summary

To get a better perspective on a number of the state and local taxes brought forth, check out the Civics lesson in the next chapter. You never would have bought this book if it were just a Civics Lesson. By the way, not all of the clever taxing schemes have been presented. We all know there are too many ways the government gets into our wallets, so we'll wrap it up for now.

However, because I am most interested in your having a good feeling for how our representatives have betrayed We the People, I offer commentary along with the Civics Lesson in the next chapter on specific taxes that you may agree are worth discussing. And if you are convinced that all should be described in a Civics Lesson, feel free to take the title of the particular tax mentioned above and place it in Google or another search engine window, and you will have your fill of explanations for and against that particular tax. Rest assured, I am against it!

The major point of this chapter is that all "representatives," and since we are all friends now, we can call them politicians, advocate for the two question simplified tax return that was credited on the Internet at the time to the Clinton Administration -- but it applies to all at all levels. The design of this Tax Return was quite simple and after it assured who you were, it had just two questions about income:

1. How much money did you make last year? _____
2. Send it in! _____

The United States has over 7,000 different taxing authorities at the state, county, and city levels. You can run but you can't hide from the US tax men. There are more taxing authorities than the size of some of the cities in which we live.

Considering that all levels of government are taxing agencies, the question arises as to whom you should send all of what you earned last year. The answer is simple: Send it to them all. If you can't figure out how to do that and it is pretty simple in theory, try to figure out how to pay your fair share of all of the many taxes that we explored in this chapter. And when you are done doing all that, if you even think you can run away from the IRS, then you may be liable to pay the Jock Tax, one of the silliest taxes of all time, if your quest for tax freedom takes you across state lines.

Chapter 10 Civics Lesson: Lots of Taxes -- Explanations

Taxes arrive in somebody's cookie jar

W. C. Fields once said to "never give a sucker an even break and never smarten up a chump!" I repeat this quip in this book because it helps to remember politicians don't want you to be smart. Are we all suckers or are we all chumps? One way we can all help ourselves is by paying attention to what the politicians are doing. If we are looking at them, when they have their hands in our cookie jars, our pockets, and our wallets, it will be more difficult for them to get away with fresh baked goods or cold hard cash.

So, let's put some text behind a few of these taxes now so that when the revenuers come visiting, you'll at least know about what they are asking.

There are a number of good Web sites and other sources available for you to find out the specifics of the various taxing states in this nation (in other words, all of them). The Web sites listed at the end of this chapter are among those that can help you in your quest for additional information. If you're curious, take a run to the end of the chapter now. Most of the URLs are short and the others can be easily found by typing the words in a search engine rather than using the long URL.

Amusement Tax

If you are amused but also sedentary, you may not owe this tax. This is a tax on the privilege of engaging in an amusement. Since politicians do not see (we think at least) what happens after the front door closes, they charge nothing for things like sweeper use, Swiffer use, pot use (cooking), watching others work, etc. etc. etc. Technically it is a tax levied on the admission price to places of amusement, entertainment, and recreation such as State Fairs, craft shows, bowling alleys, golf courses, ski facilities, or county fairs, etc. The message from your representative of course is, "Just don't be too amused or we'll get you!"

Cigarette Tax

Many states are continuing to raise excise taxes on cigarettes and other tobacco products in order to increase revenue and "cough, cough," encourage the inflicted to go on to alcohol or another abuse that won't cost the state as much. Right now, Chicago is the most expensive place to buy cigarettes. When you add the city tax, the Cook County tax and the state tax, the total tax is $3.66 per pack. Light 'em up! Smoke 'em if ya got 'em. The smoking lamp is lit on all authorized stations... Hopefully, cigarette tax revenue is being put aside because when everybody stops smoking, where will the revenue come from? Well, maybe a new vaping tax would work?

By the way, states lead the way on tobacco taxes. The American Lung Association gives the federal government an "F" for its lack of political will to impose greater taxes on tobacco. For each 10% increase in price, cigarette smoking drops by about 4%, experts say. So, why would any state look for this as a revenue source?

Earned Income Tax

Honesty has no play in this tax so if somebody says they paid it to you by giving you a W-2, you do not have to sign an affidavit that you actually earned the income. In Pennsylvania this tax is levied at the state and the municipality and the school district level. The state for example is a flat rate 3.07 and my city is 2.5 and my school district is .5 = an amount in total greater than 6%. New York state and other states have graduated income taxes as do certain cities such as, you guessed it, New York City. If you can figure out how to have revenue, but no income, I'd say you are on to something.

Emergency & Municipal Services Tax

Prior to the last ten years, this tax was often called the Occupation Privilege tax in certain states. It was a tax on the privilege of working. Only the non-workers are exempt. But, if there were a rebate on this tax, your elected would make sure the non-workers got some of your tax money "back." Wanting a means of grabbing more than the $10 or $15 this tax once generated, public servants caucused and found a much more "appropriate name" for a higher tax and in PA for one, the rate was raised to $52.00, as the maximum amount by law.

Excise Tax

Excise taxes are the government's way, without even having to accompany you on your fine dining jaunts, to know that you have it too good and it's time to share your excess with your fellow man. Technically excise taxes are general taxes paid when purchases are made on a specific good, such as gasoline. There is no emotion in that definition. The emotion comes about when you find that it is you who ultimately pays the tax.

Unlike the Jock Tax, the best part is that you don't have to keep track of these nasty taxes. These are sneaky little (maybe big if you drive an SUV) taxes that your friendly representative thinks you will blame on some "Taxing Authority" but never on your friendly representative. Collecting these taxes is simple it is almost always included in the price of the product such as in gasoline at the pump. There are lots of excise taxes because your "representatives" don't want to do anything that you will attribute to them and the notion of an excise tax sets them free from your retribution.

Fuel Tax

Try to find a state that does not collect "excise taxes" on gasoline, diesel fuel, gasohol etc., And you are destined to a continuous run through all 50 states. Enjoy the vacation. Some states charge such a high rate for fuel that when the Federal Government gives its rebates on the federal fuel charge, the politicians go out on holiday. Considering that the federal excise tax on gas is 18.4 cents and it is 24.4 cents for diesel fuel, this is more than the full price of gas was when I began to drive.

Sometime in 2008, this tax was supposed to triple, but, with the tax rebates, this idea may be dead for another year or so. When (not if) this is enacted, this increase will drive gas prices close to $4.00 per gallon. Additionally, as of now, there are nine states that, on top of the state gas tax, actually permit cities or counties to impose a local tax on fuel. What a bonanza? And you thought the oil companies were pigs?

Inheritance and Estate Taxes

If you are not rich, read the next item... Just kidding! An inheritance tax is an assessment made on the portion of an estate received by an individual. That individual may be you and that is why this entry is important. It differs from an estate tax which is a tax levied on an entire estate before it is ever distributed to individuals.

Eleven states still collect an inheritance tax. They are: Connecticut, Indiana, Iowa, Kansas, Kentucky, Maryland, Nebraska, New Jersey, Oregon, Pennsylvania and Tennessee. Connecticut will be phased out after 2005. In all states, transfers of assets to a spouse are exempt from the tax. In some states, transfers to children and close relatives are also exempt. Pennsylvanians are hoping that the Connecticut residents spared from the tax will send their savings to Governor Rendell.

As for estate taxes, in 2001 the Feds phased out the federal estate tax and it should be fully repealed in 2010 unless our representatives, and the new President find a reason to keep it a bit longer.

Don't ever trust the tax man. The estate tax is back. The scheduled but nevertheless unexpected repeal of the federal estate tax in 2010 and the prospect of its reinstatement in 2011 brought about a lot of debate over the estate tax, or "death tax." Politicians just can't give up on any tax and they proved it again.

Jock Tax

The ultimate poorly conceived tax is the "Jock Tax." This is a term that describes the original purpose of the tax. Once there is an opening for a new tax, tax authorities (a term contrived to separate our esteemed representatives from blame for their role in raising taxes) go after these new "lucrative sources" with a fervor to match a politician running for reelection.

So, why the "Jock Tax?" Quite simply, like the hotel / innkeeper tax, it seemed like an easy way for the "authorities" to cash in on what otherwise might be left to a jock / athlete to spend. And, the implication of course is, "What do they know?" In this case, it is an old tax but a new victim. States or municipalities with jock taxes noticed that traveling business professionals, particularly visiting professional athletes seemed to have some success marketing or playing basketball, football, golf, tennis etc. in their locale. So they decided to relieve them of some of the monetary reward of their success -- but just that proportion of their income earned in that state or locale.

Then, one day some politician, serving triple duty as a representative of the people and as a legislator decided that all traveling professionals should pay income taxes in every state in which they earn income or have an economic presence - regardless of how infrequently they may visit the state. So, now certain states, and more to come assess jock income taxes to visiting musicians, lawyers, skateboarders, and even touring troubadours.

Home state does not matter. These "jocks" pay their own state tax and they don't need the burden of this lousy tax. Jock taxes are unfair for sure. They represent the ultimate in poor tax policy -- poorly targeted, arbitrarily enforced, and plain greedy. Why not a tax just on politicians?

The jock tax is hard to calculate. Who decides who owes what? Can you imagine asking businessmen to justify why Cleveland should get X and Des Moines should get Y. Message to the Jock Tax aficionados, "you made a mistake. It's not a good tax." Can you imagine a salesman trying to do income tax returns for 50 states?

Mechanical Devices Tax

For those companies who choose to offer a service but yet do not offer the service via human beings, this tax applies. So, maybe now you will consider getting your own washing machine and drier rather than use coin-operated machines such as jukeboxes, pinball machines, video games, and pool tables. Maybe coin-op washing machines and driers are not eligible in all states. Maybe so? The tax rate is set as a percentage of the price to activate the machine. To avoid this tax, do not activate...

Mercantile Tax

Don't plan on selling anything to local customers or you'll pay dearly. The mercantile tax is levied on the gross receipts of local businesses selling to local consumers. Sometimes this tax is known as the business gross receipts tax, or business privilege tax. It's really not that the business pays the tax. They collect it after they raise prices to cover the tax to maintain their profit margin. Only people who never buy anything like taxes like this.

Occupation Tax

The occupation tax finds roots from England during the seventeenth and eighteenth centuries. Occupations often were a form of property which could be bought and sold, much like real estate. The tax is levied on the value of residents' occupations, as determined by the assessors office. The occupation of school bus driver may have an assessed value of $25, for example, while that of a lawyer may be $290. The school bus drivers in this case, though seeing the caste system at work in the basis for his or her lower tax, does not typically complain about the inequity.

Per Capita Tax

Only headless are exempt from this tax and so on All Hallows Eve, tax collectors have no need to visit Sleepy Hollow to capture the headless horseman. If you have a head, and you are an adult, quite simply, you pay this tax. All adults pay the same amount and knowing the mindset of bureaucrats, you probably would not be permitted to pay for more than one head.

Personal Property Tax

The ultimate gotcha is when you think they'll let you alone if you choose to do nothing and you go on a hunger strike. They will find your fine china and assess the personal property tax even if you are not using it. This tax is similar to the real property and occupation taxes in that it is levied on the value of property owned by residents. The property it taxes is typically intangible personal property, such as mortgages, other interest-bearing obligations and accounts, public loans, and corporate stocks. The personal property tax has sometimes been called an honesty tax because the only way a "taxing authority" knows the value of a taxpayer's personal property is if that taxpayer is honest enough to report it. And thus, most counties and other taxing authorities are willing to get rid of it since the reporting in this age of anything goes is a challenge.

Real Estate / Real Property Tax

This tax is a tax on the value of your real property, such as land, buildings, and other improvements, that are owned by you, making you the taxpayer. If you let the property get run down and dilapidated, your representatives will give you a tax break. But, if you use Kohler plumbing and have walls without holes, prepare to pay a big stipend to the taxing authority. What is this message?

The amount of real property tax a taxpayer owes depends upon the value of the land / improvements and the tax rate for the taxing district. Property values for tax purposes are determined by an assessment process conducted by the level of government collecting the tax though sometimes just one level does the assessment and the other levels piggyback with different rates. These assessed values are typically very different than the actual market value of the properties. Thankfully most often they are lower. So, don't use the assessed value as your appraised value.

Realty Transfer Tax

Don't even think of selling your house to put your kids through school cause they got you covered there too. The realty transfer tax is a tax on the sale of real estate. The maximum levy is whatever they decide. In PA it is 1%. PA politicians want to be fair so if both the municipality and school district levy this tax, both must share the 1 percent. Don't worry by the time you read this, the "representatives" will have plugged this loophole.

Social Security and Payroll Taxes

Since most taxpayers are tuned into the issues with the Social Security System, there is no big civics lesson associated with that topic in this book. It takes over 7.65 from most (6.2 for Social Security and 1.45 for Medicare) and 15.3% from the self-employed so it is a force to be reckoned with regarding budgeting and your gross pay. Economists suggest that those not working for someone else (not self-employed) pay the full 15.3% tax by getting lower wages.

Don't worry with the hordes of illegal aliens being paid under the table, they aren't contributing so, along with falling birthrates and rising numbers of retirees in the U.S., the future of Social Security is described by our representatives at best as "uncertain." But it really is certain. It is doomed unless a few more Warren Buffets surface and they choose to donate to the cause.

Over the years, tax economists have published many studies exploring Social Security's financial problems and outlining possible reforms to help restore the system to long-term solvency. Since our "representatives" do not have to pay heed to sound recommendations, the problem has gotten worse and unless we change the makeup of our government, it will get even worse. Besides all that, our representatives have permitted stealing from the fund to pay other bills over the years and that has made the situation even more difficult because none of the borrowers at any level of government have paid anything back.

State Sales Tax

All states except Alaska, Delaware, Montana, New Hampshire and Oregon, collect sales taxes. But to go there just for that might be too expensive. Maybe it is a good deal if you're thinking of buying your next yacht. OK, no more dreaming. Some states charge one percentage rate throughout the state though most states permit local additions to the base tax rate. No locations as of today have offered deductions. States with no local add-on include Connecticut, Hawaii, Indiana, Kentucky, Maine, Maryland, Massachusetts, Michigan, Mississippi, New Jersey, Rhode Island, Vermont, Virginia, and West Virginia. The Big sales tax state is California (7.25%). Mississippi clocks in with New Jersey and Tennessee and Rhode Island at 7% while Minnesota and Nevada at 6.5% are waiting for the Taxpayer

Foundation to go on vacation to get their rates to the top. Cash registers calculate this stuff so easily that "representatives" will figure out how to take a tax over the years that is already too much and make it render even more. . And, you know where that all comes from -- right?

Sources:

- Federation of Tax Administrators; http://www.taxadmin.org/
- MSN Money "The Best and Worst States for taxes"; http://articles.moneycentral.msn.com/Taxes/Advice/TheBestAndWorstStatesForTaxes.aspx
- National Conference of State Legislatures; http://www.ncsl.org/
- Retirement Living Information Center; http://www.retirementliving.com/RLtaxes.htm
- Sales Tax Clearinghouse http://thestc.com/
- State Tax Handbook; http://www.amazon.com/State-Tax-Handbook-Timothy-Bjur/dp/0808015362
- The Tax Foundation; http://www.taxfoundation.org/
- U.S. Department of Commerce, Bureau of Economic Analysis; http://www.bea.gov/
- Various state tax and revenue departments; Use search engine

Chapter 11 Americans: Overtaxed & Under Represented

Representatives do not do their jobs

We are taxed more than ever before today and just as in 1776, there is no sign of real representation. We go through the motions of holding elections regularly but then those who occupy the highest government offices choose to represent themselves and their families rather than the people of the US.

The spirit and reality of representative government that once enlivened this country following the American Revolution has all but eroded into what we see today: an ad hoc litany of superficial homage to the discarded bedrock of what was once the very foundation of this great country.

I wrote this book because our representatives in the House, the Senate, in state legislatures and city councils have forgotten their duties as representatives of the people. Additionally, the president, the governors, the mayors, and other prefects of the people in the executive branches of governments across the land have conveniently forgotten that the primary fundamentals of our representative constitutional democracy (republic) begin with representation.

No single branch of government can claim immunity in the sale and resale of the United States to outside interests and American corporations. Each knows no moral bound or impediment to the gluttonous drive to perpetuate its self-serving two-party system. Even the judiciary is more caught up in preserving the two-party system than permitting deserving independents their opportunity to run for public office.

All of the candidates running for president in 2008, for example, called for big changes. They were all right. They struck a chord with the American people on "hope" and "change," but none offered specifics. Barack Obama came from no-place to be the cheerleader in charge and now, eight years later it is clear that he moved the country so far to the left that the center is barely visible. Donald Trump is helping us get the other end of spectrum in focus. So far he has been successful.

Nobody seemed to know what was on Mr. Obama's agenda. But we all learned fast enough with Obamacare as his top issue along with its big mess of poor options, higher fees, higher taxes, and poor medical care that we were in trouble as a nation. The preponderance of thought was that the President's to-do-list was created by his Chicago cronies, including Reverend Wright, Father Pfleger, and the followers of the master of indoctrination and quiet insurrection, Saul Alinsky.

As we emerged from the 2016 election cycle, we found that Hillary Clinton had promised four more years of Barck Obama's policies and more of Alinsky. Saul Alinsky was Hillary's favorite prophet from back when she was a kid and George Soros is still her favorite benefactor.

How bad can it get?

Right now, at the termination point of Obama's eight very long years of OJT, and with a new president working fast to undue the harm, we no longer appear to be headed like a missile down a road from which we may not be able to return.

In the Obama years, there was a major assault on individualism, the Constitution, capitalism, and democracy itself, in favor of socialism and perhaps even Marxism (Bernie Sanders) and non-violent Communism. We need only look to England in colonial times to see how bad it can get in all aspects of life—at least for freedom lovers. Keep your muskets loaded at night for sure.

The irony of the last two elections before this one, is that as the people asked for real change, they counted on honest and skilled people, not self-centered ideologues to get the job done for them. We reap what we sow. Many today admit that they sowed poorly in those past election choices.

The greatest enemy of a skilled corrupt politician is an informed public. Therefore, it is always time to learn, learn, and learn! This is a good book to begin your efforts. After what we have seen in the last few years, an informed public would be very careful about putting a skilled corrupt politician in any position of consequence.

Despite our best efforts, we were duped about political intentions in 2008 and again in 2012 because the "free press" is in the hip pocket of at least one of the political parties. The press is free to be corrupt and lie about whatever it likes. One day, we will learn not to pay any heed to their message.

We went to the Senate and it seemed out of 100 people, all anybody could find were Hillary Clinton, John McCain and Barack Obama. Did we really think the Senate was doing that great a job for us to pick our president from its "esteemed membership?"

The final Democrat (Obama) and Republican (McCain) were already in the symbolic House of Lords. Americans choose to call it the Senate, but it has become the House of Lords once again, and nobody from this body should have made it even to the candidate stage. They are the elite establishment and they have chosen no longer to represent the people. They live separated from the people and the breather only the rarified air available to the chosen.

Choose carefully always, when you vote

Representation at all levels for the most part is non-existent, and yet we are being taxed more and more. If we do not change our government now, with better people for the 535 positions available in the full six-year election cycle, there will be little chance for better representation until 2022. Sending corrupt Senators back to office or rewarding them with a better position (Presidency) is not the right thing for Americans to do.

Our representative democracy and its Constitution together are known as a republic form of government. A republic has nothing to do with *Republican* other than the first eight letters. Living in a republic however does not make any of us Republicans. A republic is simply a representative democracy with a set of rules known as a Constitution so that the politicians cannot decide to enrich themselves instead of taking care of the people.

In the 2008 and 2012 election seasons, from which we are still recovering, there were few Americans who had not tuned into the problems we faced. Yet, we were not looking to overthrow our republic with a dictatorship.

We should have taken more time figuring out who the candidates really were. This change has cost us dearly as the status quo was clearly better for us and our children before the "big change." Thankfully, this negative change is being reversed by President Trump as things were about ready to get a lot worse and may never have gotten better with four more years that were like the last eight.

We had eight long years of an unresponsive presidency with a weak-kneed Congress. They gave us unprotected borders and an unprotected America vulnerable to terrorist attacks at a terrorist's whim. In all of this we had a President apologizing for America all over the world for upsetting terrorists.

Our Congress continues to be dysfunctional as the Democrats are prepared to destroy America rather than agree to a tax break for the middle class. Republicans are still weak. They do not want to be blamed for anything and so for almost all of 2017, they did nothing.

The whole scenario in Washington – the guys we sent to represent us—is still fraught with infighting, back-stabbing, and blame games seemingly peeled from the script pages of a discarded low-budget sitcom, except for one thing.

After we got the change "we can believe in," most can't believe we got that kind of change. The economy went right into the toilet and it has been there for eight years. Freedom was being attacked on all fronts, more than any time ever in most of our lifetimes. Only now, in the first year of the Trump administration is the economy showing signs of real life.

The result of wishing for, and getting the Obama administration to exert its change on freedom loving people would be funny if it had not been so dire in its reality. For years, many of the older generation would joke when somebody would complain that Congress and the administration had gotten nothing done. Their quip was always: "Good." In the Bush years nothing done was the modus operandi.

In the Obama years, it was scary how quickly the former president ushered the entire country into the poor-house. We became a well-taxed and poorly represented group looking for leadership and not finding any. Some joked in the Bush years that it was good that nothing was getting done since at least it meant that the corporations weren't getting any further ahead of us.

With Obama mowing people down regularly wherever his notions are deployed, finding big government as his only answer, we were soon longing for the days of plain old corporate dominance.

Things have not been going well for us

The report card is already finished on Obama and the legislative branches for the past eight years. It is definitely not good. We should not be sending any one of our legislators back to do anything "for us" ever. For the last ten years, our country has been sold out. Congress's 14% approval rating today is too high for the job they are doing.

Actually, it's a lot more than ten, from Obama back through Bush past the Clintons to the last Bush. For twenty plus years there was no real progress for the good of the people while the establishment and the elites became more entrenched and harder to unseat. Additionally, the state of affairs has gotten substantially worse. Government become even more dominant, corrupt, and downright neglectful and disrespectful towards the people.

Those in power need to be held accountable: No repeat performances and no repeat performers. American prosperity has been sold down the tubes as jobs and national secrets and intellectual property have gone overseas and labor arbitrage (get to the lowest wage quickly) is the order of the day for non-union workers at home while union jobs move overseas.

There are few ordinary citizens better off today than the day Ronald Reagan left office. This country does need change. It must be a change for the better. Your author in this book outlines many areas in which we all can make big improvements. Step one of course begins with full government accountability and an untrusting public.

Though charged with the duty to represent the people, public servants are so overwhelmed with self-interests, special interests, the interests of corporations and the interests of other countries that they have no time to work for the people. When you finish reading this book, you will see that the "honorables" are not serving America honorably.

Taxation is OK with representation

"No taxation without representation" was the catch phrase in the period of 1763-1776 to summarize the major grievance of the American colonists in the Thirteen American Colonies, incipient kernels of what would later become the United States of America.

When King George III of England and the English Parliament began to impose new taxes on the colonists (Stamp Act, Intolerable Acts, etc.) without their concurrence, Reverend Jonathan Mayhew of Boston coined this term during one of his sermons in Boston.

Another Bostonian, a politician by *the speak of the day,* James Otis, changed this just a bit and he is well known for the phrase, "taxation without representation is tyranny." Tyranny it was, and in this book, you will see that tyranny, it surely is again.

In 1773, American Colonists violently opposed the tax on tea imports at the most celebrated Tea Party of all time. The Boston Tea Party is recognized as the first experience in which the colonists acted against the Crown. Of course, the British could not accept this "illegal act" as they saw that it would undermine the authority of the Crown and Parliament. When the British Government began to crack down on these "illegal activities" as performed by the colonists, the colonists chose to defend themselves in case the British Government did not hear their pleas to correct the abuses.

Though today the tea still may be gone from the ships in Boston Harbor, millions have expressed outrage for our government for the last eight years and then some. Just a few years ago, the notion of the Tea Party was used to show the people's rage. This was a national movement.

Conservative Americans from all over the country held Tea Party rallies in protest against the American government and rampant corruption in Washington. The corrupt press maligned the conservatives who joined in these rallies and nobody talks about tea anymore though the same spirit is in the streets of America. Bernie Sanders and Donald Trump awakened the spirit of "NO" to a government that began to think that owned the people of this great nation.

Why no representation?

Just like the British Crown, today's Parliament and the Crown (Congress & the President) have demeaned the efforts of the new colonists (We the people of 2018) to get their word across the nation. The demonstrators of the new millennium may not have thrown real tea in the ocean, but they were all nonetheless maligned as Astroturfers, and simply as an "angry" mob by the Queen of Mean, House leader Pelosi, and former president Obama himself. The people were very unsettled and responded by electing Donald Trump, a non-politico with more savvy than all 535 in our Congress.

So, in addition to all the ills suffered under Bush, who pretended to be conservative, the elected change to Obama as the chief executive brought forth government attacks on free speech and individual initiative, and freedom itself. The people were not about to let this stand. Enter Donald J. Trump.

Where are our representatives? One would believe they are hiding as they are spotted only rarely at election time. Regardless of Party, they all seemed to have joined to be in unison with a former president who had little respect for Americans. The supposed representatives of the people have committed acts against the people by supporting the perverted Obama agenda for eight years and despite the poor results, they show no remorse. This is unprecedented in history. Now that we have the presidency in good hands, it is time to send the representatives packing on the next train out of Washington.

Colonists & regular people—tough indeed!

During the revolution, the brave colonists, not willing to be taxed without representation, formed militias and took control of each of the thirteen colonies. They armed themselves and expelled the Crown-appointed governors and they began an independence process for the new states of what would become the United States of America.

I am not suggesting that a physical revolution is now in order, but it may be time for actually dumping a spot of tea in Boston Harbor or a harbor near you. Perhaps a few teapots worth of brew would symbolize that it is time to take America back from the political class, the establishment that Donald Trump has so incensed, and from those corrupt politicians (the SWAMP), who do not respect our democracy.

Patrick Henry, Ben Franklin, Thomas Jefferson, George Washington, John Adams, John Hancock, Paul Revere, and many other brave Patriots helped create a more perfect union of states despite the personal hardships they endured and the major risks that they took.

The cry of the colonists against Great Britain was not that high taxes were being exacted. Actually, the taxes were minimal. The issue was the fact that the taxes and everything else about the colonies were decided in London, and there were *no representatives* of the colonies permitted to be heard.

This is in so many ways the cry from the Elites and the establishment from the blood lines in Washington to give up the country to those who have ruled quietly behind the scenes. Maybe if these "quiet" rulers actually wanted what was best for the people, the people would not object. But their actions are not for the people. They are for their own selfish selves. It is amazing that when the people called for a Trump, the moneyed class said "NO," and yet somehow, with no money, the people won. When the people pay attention, we cannot be beaten. We have the votes that count.

And, so, it can be said that it was the pure desire for full freedom, and the annoyances from a lack of representation from the elected constabulary, that was the big issue for the colonists. We have the same issues today. It is not the taxation. It is the lack of representation. The people no longer feel that we can trust the government and we no longer trust that our representatives work for our best interests.

After the revolution, George Washington accepted British General Cornwallis's surrender and as noted previously, the congress wanted him to be King. During the Revolutionary War, the Founding Fathers ran the affairs of government using the Articles of Confederation while they were working on a better way—the Constitution.

When the representatives of the thirteen colonies of the United States put together their beliefs about how things were to be in the future, this august body codified their thoughts into one of the most wonderful documents ever written. As we all know, this almost-perfect document is known as the Constitution of the United States of America. It was put forth in order to create a *more perfect* union of the states compared with the Articles of Confederation, which was their first try.

The Constitution itself as difficult as it is to believe was continually attacked by the Obama administration on numerous occasions.

The Constitution of the United States delineates that the purpose of the government is to be--by, for, and of--the citizens of the United States. Corporations are not mentioned in the Constitution as citizens or unfeeling creatures or entities of any kind. Why? It was simply because the colonists and the Founding Fathers had great disdain for corporations. The last thing on their minds was to build a new government to please these huge fictitious abstractions.

Representation of the people was paramount in the founders' minds. These were the framers of the Constitution. They decided that the country would be formed from three separate branches of government—executive (President), legislative (Congress), and judicial (Supreme Court and the normal Judiciary). This form of government under the Constitution has endured to this day but it is definitely having its challenges, as the men / women in the official roles in Washington do not seem to respect the precepts that the founding fathers had so ordained.

With 5 million people living in the colonies back then, it would have been difficult to fit all 5 million into the same church basement or town hall to conduct the needed affairs of the government. So, a strict direct democracy was not feasible, and the form of our government became a representative democracy with a governing set of rules known as a Constitution. As noted previously, this is the definition of a republic.

As you read this book, you will find a number of identified Civics Lessons, which provide the reader with the knowledge to see how our government was formed and how it operates and how it taxes. The lessons also demonstrate how our Congress and our President, especially our immediate past president, have been changing it de-facto to suit their needs.

Their methods would be declared unconstitutional if brought before an unbiased court that was truly interested in adjudicating grievances according to the law and not according to their biased ideology.

Influential corporations, the former president and too many other politicians were playing on the same team against the people. Corporations act together in an organized way so they can buy a Congress and by owning the press, they can buy public opinion very cheaply.

They are out actively buying up enough of both Congress and public opinion to serve their own selfish interests. Notice how wages are falling and jobs are disappearing and yet the political class and the press parrot that things are better. The elite business class and the Congress, which they control, have been systematically lowering wages and blaming circumstances beyond their control. Since they own Congress, and the media, it has been very easy.

If it isn't our Senators and House members and the President who have betrayed us, then who is it? Our leaders have forgotten that they work for the people and not vice versa. You can see the signs of a government unresponsive to its people in regard to a number of major issues such as the unbridled rise of corporate power, the rise of government power, Obamacare, the giveaway of American jobs to those in other countries as well as jobs for legal and illegal foreign nationals, undefended borders and the intrusion of illegal aliens into all aspects of American life and the associated costs to the citizenry.

Seanotors must face the people in elections once every six years; Congress once every two years, and the president, once every four years. In six years, we can replace them all. The logical conclusion is to throw the bums out or else we will keep getting the government we deserve as we elect them again and again.

Chapter 12 The Rise of Corporate Power

The Union is not perfect

Merriam Webster defines capitalism as an economic system characterized by private or corporate ownership of capital goods, by investments that are determined by private decision, and by prices, production, and the distribution of goods that are determined mainly by competition in a free market. In the "Logic of Action, 1997" Murray N. Rothbard defines state capitalism as consisting of

> "one or more groups making use of the coercive apparatus of the government... for themselves by expropriating the production of others by force and violence."

In the eight long years of President Obama, there was a lot of crony capitalism which, as we have learned from Rothbard and others, is an aberration of capitalism, specifically, an economic system characterized by close, mutually advantageous relationships between business leaders and government officials. Today, Rothbard's groups are corporations that in one way or another have an unholy alliance with government and receive assistance or approval for their "work" from the government and they receive favorable legislation from our representatives.

And you thought this was not going to be a fun book? One of the problems that we have today in the US, and one of the many in which our elected representatives have taken a pass is the increasingly negative notion of the corporation. At this point, I am not talking just about corporate greed.

Corporations are now citizens

The theme of this chapter is much more basic than stopping corporate greed. A quick read of the Constitution and you will not see anything about Corporations as quasi-citizens or having any legitimate right to exist. The Founding Fathers hated the mere idea of corporations as they had seen their impact on England.

Because of their disdain for corporations, one would not expect to find any rights for such entities in our early documents and in fact, there are none. Nonetheless, the greedy and the powerful, who are often one and the same, have managed to change the intent of the founders in a way that even they would not have imagined.

In their present form, there is so much abuse and potential for abuse that perhaps corporations should wholesale be eliminated. But, before they are fully gone, a citizens' board needs to watch over their predatory actions against the population, and after they are gone, their assets need to be distributed to "companies" equitably, if that is even possible.

So, we are all on the same page, let's take a quick look at what makes up a corporation. What exactly is a corporation?

A corporation is a nonhuman entity. It is a fictitious citizen because it has no meat and bones, but it has received over time the power to operate in most other ways as a citizen. In fact, corporations have some attributes, such as stock issuance that a citizen does not have or need. Investor Words provides us with this definition

> A corporation is the most common form of business organization, and one which is chartered by a state and given many legal rights as an entity separate from its owners. This form of business is characterized by the *limited liability* of its owners, the issuance of shares of easily transferable *stock*, and existence as a *going concern*.
>
> The process of becoming a corporation, called incorporation, gives the company separate legal standing from its owners and protects those owners from being personally liable in the event that the company is sued (a condition known as limited liability).
>
> Incorporation also provides companies with a more flexible way to manage their ownership structure. In addition, there are different *tax* implications for corporations, although these can be both

advantageous and disadvantageous. In these respects, corporations differ from *sole proprietorships* and *limited partnerships*.

Before we begin to discuss the numerous reasons why corporations are built to get out of control and are absolutely out of control, let's take a few pokes at the government of the United States from more than 200 years ago. The first notion that helped corporations become implied citizens came about in the Marbury v. Madison case of 1803. Please note that the current Supreme Court and the Executive offices are not the first to have played with our Constitution.

This case established the concept of judicial review, which sounds like an OK thing, but it tips the balance of power of the three levels of government to the Supreme Court. The founding fathers never intended a tipping of the balance. In 1803, the Supreme Court ruled that they were "Supreme" and the Congress at the time did not fully evaluate what this meant and the fools (IMHO) did not contest it.

This, in essence gave the Supreme Court the power to make law. Oh, they can't propose legislation, and have it voted upon per se, but this small group of nine got the power from an unawake Congress to divine the "real intentions" of the authors of any law upon which they get to rule, even if the law had nothing to do with their divinations.

Using its power to divine intent -- even the intent of the Constitution, in 1889, in the Minneapolis & St. Louis Railroad Co. v. Beckwith case, the Supreme Court, in one of its worst rulings of all time, declared that a corporation is a person for both due process and equal protection under the process.

Since Shakespeare's time It's been argued that "something is rotten in the state of Denmark." The 1889 Supreme Court decision helped begin the decay of the potential for the American dream, unless, of course, you have no flesh. And that, my dear readers is a travesty. The damage is done but it must be undone. After eight years, even the Obama czars could not steal away all of our rights. The people still have the power, and we need to act judiciously through the Congress to make this right again.

Money, corporations and the ruling class

Because of all the money that passes through corporations, the ruling class through their corporate power, have more rights than the people. This commonly accepted notion of a corporation, that it is like a person, goes way too far and shifts the power from sovereign individuals. If we were a country in which ethics and morals were the guiding principles—as when we were founded—this would not be such a bad deal for the people.

It was bad in 1889 with the "Robber Barons," but today, in the "me" generation, ethics and morals often are not even afforded lip service. Today in fact, the blatant greed of corporations and their owners is ever visible as one worker after another is losing his or her jobs to lower paid foreigners, and one corrupt corporate officer after another is being indicted for violating the public trust.

In my home town of Luzerne County, PA, Pennsylvania judges and other politicos are going to jail after careers of stiffing their constituencies. The fact that they have been indicted and have been convicted in many cases actually is a major sign of hope.

As hopeful as we may be, in the great bailouts of 2008 and 2009, the principle that a corporate entity might be too big to fail has become something of which to be concerned. Check the Constitution and you will find nothing that says the people are to bail out poorly run corporations merely because they can't make a buck in a free market.

Yet, for the longest time, the Obama government owns General Motors and Chrysler and a good many of the nation's financial institutions.

You may recall that on July 10, 2009, General Motors came out of government backed Chapter 11 reorganization after an initial filing on June 8, 2009. The Troubled Asset Relief Program of the US Treasury (Too big to fail), invested $49.5 billion in General Motors and recovered $39 billion when it sold its shares on December 9, 2013 resulting in a loss of $10.3 billion. The US lost $10.3 Billion on its running of GM for four years.

The Treasury also invested another $17.2 billion into GM's former financing company, GMAC (now Ally). These shares were sold on December 18, 2014 for $19.6 billion netting $2.4 billion. People rave about the government saving GM but I see it differently. GM had so many intellectual assets, brands, and hard assets that it could have been sold outright or broken up into nice neat divisions and sold, and the government's stinky paws could have been kept out of the picture. Government's job is not to help corporations. Check the Constitution. When was the last time a corporation helped you when you were short of funds?

Obama's government also saw fit to immerse itself in Chrysler's operations and bailout. Did America really need Chrysler when Ford was doing fine, and GM had gotten bailed out. Nonetheless, on June 10, 2009, substantially all of Chrysler's assets were sold to "New Chrysler", organized as Chrysler Group LLC.

The federal government operating as a big kind brother, with no Constitutional authority to do so, provided $8 billion in financing. On May 24, 2011, Chrysler repaid its $7.6 billion loans to the United States and Canadian governments. The US Treasury, through the Troubled Asset Relief Program (TARP), invested $12.5 billion in Chrysler and recovered $11.2 billion when the company shares were sold in May 2011, resulting in a $1.3 billion loss.

On July 21, 2011, Fiat bought the Chrysler shares held by the US Treasury. The purchase made Chrysler foreign-owned again, this time as the luxury division. So, in order to save Chrysler, the Taxpayers bailed them out with over a $billion loss, and Chrysler is no longer a US company. Tell me why this could not have happened naturally if we had just let Chrysler, a poorly performing company simply fail? What would be different?

And, then of course there were the banks and Wall Street, another government boondoggle to put taxpayer money into the pockets of Obama cronies. It has been eight long winters since the federal government, by the hand of then-Treasury Secretary Hank Paulson, gave $700 billion in taxpayer money to rescue Wall Street from its own chicanery and greed. I don't remember any thank-you cards for this gift from taxpayers to crooks.

The bankers seem to believe to this day (ahem!) along with lobbyists and allies in Washington that the bailout was the best thing to hit the American economy since the industrial revolution. They even claim that the money has paid back – but to whom?
It is all a lie, a big lie for sure but a lie that regular normal people could not decipher. We were told that the taxpayer was stepping in – only temporarily, mind you – to prop up the economy and save the world from financial catastrophe.

What we got was the opposite – an eternity of committing American taxpayers to permanent, blind support of an ungovernable, unregulatable, too-powerful, new financial system that made greed more popular and brought back the same inequality that caused the original crash. The people thought we were just letting a friend crash at the house for a few days; but we wound up with a family of hillbillies who moved in forever, sleeping nine to a bed and selling drugs on the front lawn. What can government do right? Healthcare? Get out of town!

By not adhering to the principles of survival of the fittest, the action of our government has blessed a future in which these major corporations and others too big to fail have a built-in permanent weakness. They do not have to excel to exceed. They can actually fail again and use the people's treasury to bail them out while lining their pockets with cash. This means that the rich ruling class no longer have to risk their capital to succeed. They now risk ours as held by the US Treasury, and this must end now.

Exxon the money machine

By the way, in the 1990's IBM lost $13 billion. Nobody bailed IBM out but itself. It was quite devastating for IBM and Mr. Akers, the Chairman. Yet, it is nothing compared with Exxon's single quarter profits. In February 2008 the oil giant made corporate history by logging in a sweet $11.7 billion for just three month's work. That is some sweet corporate citizen. Meanwhile Americans were choking up cash from coffee cans to pay for gasoline.

The math majors quickly translated the Exxon profit news for the John Doe's out here by noting that its 2007 earnings could also be stated as $1,300 a second. Before the huge executive salaries payoffs and other company expenses were subtracted, the company grossed about $350 billion for the year.

$45.22 Billion Profit for 2008

In my wildest dreams when I wrote the first edition of this book, I could not see revenues topping $400,000,000,000 in 2008. Hey, as life got more miserable for the taxpayer, in 2008, the economy busting excessive gas and oil prices had a huge impact on Exxon. Even those who predicted good times, never saw how the corporate greed factor could ever pull in such unbelievable record revenue of $477,851,000,000 for 2008. In my humble opinion, these record profits began the economic downfall that assured a Republican defeat and assured Barack Obama's victory as change was definitely needed.

Exxon stock is up again in October 2017 by nearly 1 percent at $84.25 in pre-market trading. In the latest, the oil major earned 93 cents per share on $66.16 billion in revenue. Analysts had expected earnings of 86 cents a share on $63.39 billion ($63,390,000,000) in revenues. In the year ago period, Exxon earned 63 cents per share on $58.68 billion in revenues. Forget about ever taking an inexpensive Sunday drive again.

Corporations and government collusion

Though I once listened daily as the former Commander in Chief appeared even more petulant in the news proselytizing his agenda for destroying America, I heard nary a whimper about the evils of corporations -- oil or otherwise. Yet, I have saw much of the national treasury dumped out for those corporations that had no idea of how to be successful.

If I were able to check further, I am sure I would find wads of cash from contrived payoff business deals heading for the treasuries of the corporations that helped the former president get elected. Using the people's treasury to pay off huge corporations seems to be an acceptable practice nowadays, though it is blatantly dishonest. The wallets of the corporate titans are wide open so that they can be filled by government largess.

FYI, government largess is where liberals take away our money to give it to "the needy" (such as GM and Wall Street) in ways that make current elected officials appear generous. Generally, these acts of generosity are given in ways that undermine the recipient's abilities to survive without government generosity.

In my IBM career, I recall that IBM once grossed more than Exxon. IBM is now about a $79 billion-dollar company and Exxon, which at one time was $477 billion when gas prices were through the roof, and now is just about $200 billion but profits are screaming. Meanwhile Apple, a company that made just a few million when it made PCs before IBM, when IBM dominated IT sales, now checks in with over $230 billion per year in revenue

Way back when the government often worked for the people, it took it upon itself to sue IBM because it was a monopoly. Somehow as big as it was, it was OK for Exxon to acquire Mobil Oil and yet they still have not yet been tagged a monopoly -- and until recently, this was a democratic administration. What gives?

Corporations have no heart and no blood

In his article of the *unofficial history of America*, Kalle Lasn captures the essence of corporations from time immemorial at least from a U.S. perspective. He notes that there are official and unofficial versions of the fight against the Crown. In his unofficial version he identifies a real and true perpetrator of far more consequence than the flesh-laden robber barons, but in the same ilk. These are the English corporations, who operated in America during the pre-revolution days, and who in many ways helped contribute to the colonists frustration with England. Corporations of old helped prompt the colonists desire to be completely free of the Crown as well as its corporate allies. Lasn writes:

> ... The unofficial history of the United States is quite different. It begins the same way -- in the revolutionary cauldron of colonial America -- but then it takes a turn. A bit player in the official history becomes critically important to the way the

unofficial history unfolds. This player turns out to be not only the provocateur of the revolution, but in the end its saboteur. This player lies at the heart of America's defining theme: the difference between a country that pretends to be free and a country that truly is free.

That player is the corporation.

The United States of America was born of a revolt not just against British monarchs and the British parliament but against British corporations.

We tend to think of corporations as a fairly recent phenomenon, along with the legacy of the Rockefellers and Carnegies. In fact, the corporate presence in pre-Revolutionary America was almost as conspicuous as it is today. There were far fewer corporations then, but they were enormously powerful: the Massachusetts Bay Company, the Hudson's Bay Company, and the British East India Company numbered among their ranks. Colonials feared these chartered entities. They recognized the way British Kings and their cronies used them as robotic arms to control the affairs of the colonies, to pinch staples from remote breadbaskets and bring them home to the motherland.

The colonials resisted. When the British East India Company imposed duties on its incoming tea (telling the locals they could buy the tea or lump it, because the company had a virtual monopoly on tea distribution in the colonies), radical patriots demonstrated. Colonial merchants agreed not to sell East India Company tea. Many East India Company ships were turned back at port. And, on one fateful day in Boston, 342 chests of tea ended up in the salt chuck.

... The Declaration of Independence, in 1776, freed Americans not only from Britain but also from the tyranny of British corporations, and for a hundred years after the document's signing, Americans remained deeply suspicious of corporate power. They were careful about the way they granted corporate charters, and about the powers granted therein.

... Early American charters were created literally by the people, for the people as a legal convenience. Corporations were "artificial, invisible, intangible," mere financial tools. They were chartered by individual states, not the federal government, which meant they could be kept under close local scrutiny. They were automatically dissolved if they engaged in activities that violated their charter. Limits were placed on how big and powerful companies could become. Even railroad magnate J. P. Morgan, the consummate capitalist, understood that corporations must never become so big that they "inhibit freedom to the point where efficiency [is] endangered."

The two hundred or so corporations operating in the US by the year 1800 were each kept on fairly short leashes. They weren't allowed to participate in the political process. They couldn't buy stock in other corporations. And if one of them acted improperly, the consequences were severe.

In 1832, President Andrew Jackson vetoed a motion to extend the charter of the corrupt and tyrannical Second Bank of the United States, and was widely applauded for doing so. That same year the state of Pennsylvania revoked the charters of ten banks for operating contrary to the public interest. Even the enormous industry trusts, formed to protect member corporations from external competitors and provide barriers to entry, eventually proved no match for the state. By the mid-1800s, antitrust legislation was widely in place.

... The shift began in the last third of the nineteenth century -- the start of a great period of struggle between corporations and civil society. The turning point was the Civil War. Corporations made huge profits from procurement contracts and took advantage of the disorder and corruption of the times to buy legislatures, judges and even presidents.

A larger excerpt of *The Unofficial History of America*, is available on the Web for your pleasure at:
/www.informationclearinghouse.info/article3925.htm

Looks like a good book to buy after you finish this one.

Thank you Kalle Lasn for a great account of the early corporations in the United States. Clearly the wary eye of the government of the states was needed to keep corporate power in check so that nothing like the British East India Company could ever rise again to terrify the citizens of the U. S. A.

Unfortunately, through political greed and individual greed, corporations have re-gained a foothold in the U.S. that will be very difficult to un-foot. Looking back, one thing is clear. Ours is not the first generation to have been exploited by corporations in concert with dirty politicians and ours will not be the last. But, it sure would be nice if we could do something about it.

Brief history of corporations

Joel Bleifuss in his article "*A Brief History of Corporations*" In <u>These Times</u> magazine, February 1998 minces no words as he outlines the issues with corporations and then speaks about how ridiculous it is that we permit their very being:

> To begin this retooling process, we need to expose the absurdity of granting First Amendment rights to corporations. We can draw our inspiration from both the 17th-century English philosopher Thomas Hobbes, who decried corporations as "worms in the body politic," and from Hobbes' star pupil, King Charles II. In 1664, the owners of the Massachusetts Bay Company protested when Charles II tried to investigate their company's operations. The Crown responded, "The King did not grant away his sovereignty over you when he made you a corporation.... When his majesty gave you authority over such subjects as live within your jurisdiction, he made them not your subjects, nor you their supreme authority."

We should be as wise.

http://query.nytimes.com/gst/fullpage.html?res=9F02EEDE173DF937A25752C1A96F958260&sec=&spon=&pagewanted=all

Peter F. Drucker died about six years after being referenced in a New York times article in the URL above. He is forever revered as the father of modern management. In 1999, he had a new message for corporate executives: "Find another line of work." In this book, for this insight and the hope that it comes true, we must say, "Bravo! Dr. Drucker"

Drucker saw the information and knowledge workers today as retreating from corporate culture and instead saving their best efforts for nonprofit social service organizations, where he felt that in the 21st century, they could make a bigger difference. In his words, "The 20th century was the century of business," he said. "The next century is going to be the century of the social sector." So, again there is hope... as long as it does not turn to full socialism.

Abolish corporations? -- an opinion

http://ming.tv/flemming2.php/ show_article/ a000010-000393.htm

Flemming Funch, perhaps a pseudonym for a guy who does not want to be identified, offers a number of insights and caveats as to how to abolish corporations. He believes that the biggest obstacle blocking the emergence of a free and peaceful world is the legal concept of a corporation. He notes that the corporation as we have discussed is merely a legal fiction in the first place, and it is "not any naturally occurring 'god-given' phenomenon or right."

Corporations exist only because our representatives, against the known wishes of the founders, have made laws saying that they can exist and they have rights only because again our representatives in the legislature and in the courts have said they have rights.

Funch recognizes that the notion of the corporation per se would be hard to eliminate because just like anything about to die, the corporation would fight like hell to survive and they would use their vast resources to protect and even expand their own power. Bribing our elected officials is certainly one of their favorite armaments. Here is Funch:

People should certainly be able to organize themselves and operate as a group or organization. But a corporation is something else. A corporation is allowed the rights of a natural person. However, it has responsibilities and liabilities less than a natural person. And it can live eternally.

These things can be useful and sensible when it is a small group of people who are trying to operate a business activity together. The initial people don't have to be too worried about being personally liable for the potential failure of the business, and the business can open a bank account for itself, and it can be continued even if the original participants drop out for some reason.

But when it grows bigger, there are certain key design features that start to become prevalent. A corporation is controlled by very few people, but the fuel is provided by a great many people, in the form of investments and manpower.

A large corporation might have the will of one person, carrying out one person's plans, and it has the legal right to act in most arenas as one legal person, but it might have the manpower of 100,000 people, and available resources bigger than those of a small country. All in the hands of a handful of people who don't have any personal liability for what the corporation does.

It is very difficult to successfully convey what a horribly bad idea that is. Most of us are so used to the idea of corporations, and most of us have bought the propaganda that they're inextricably linked to free markets. Nothing could be further from the truth. Large multi-national corporations are the antithesis of free markets. They are the communist revolution you never even noticed happening.

A big corporation is much like a communist state, or like an old-fashioned kingdom with a divinely ordained dictatorial ruler, if you like that metaphor better. If you are one of its subjects, it might take good care of you, feeding you and clothing you, and it might give you bonuses and parties and fancy titles.

But you have to do what you're told, and you have to direct your efforts to the benefit of the will of your rulers. It is not a democracy in any way. You have no rights whatsoever in terms of influencing what it does or how it does it, other than within the confines of the job you've been assigned from someone higher up in the hierarchy.

But as an employee it isn't too bad, just like it wasn't terribly bad for most people to live in a communist country. Your range of success is very limited, but you can feel fairly secure that you'll have a job if you continue to do what you're told, and you can be confident that it doesn't matter a whole lot what you individually do or don't do.

... playing in the market with large corporations is typically not fair. The CEO of a large corporation can book every single billboard in town, pay for TV infomercials, hire experts of all sorts, all to say exactly what he wants to say, very loudly, so that everyone in sight will hear it, again, and again and again.

Chapter 13 The Robber Barons Are Back

Corporations often hide the Barons

There are many who believe in their hearts and many others who have actual proof that the "Robber Baron" days are back again but this time the human perpetrators are not being identified since a corporate veil hides them from public scrutiny -- unless they get too greedy. So, unlike the 1890s we do not see names of heralded industrial leaders such as John D. Rockefeller (pictured as King of the world in Figure 13-1 below courtesy of usinfo.state.gov.), Cornelius Vanderbilt, Grenville Dodge, Leland Stanford, Henry Villard, James J. Hill, and others who in the days before the 20th century got that nasty label, "Robber Barons."

Figure 13-1 Standard Oil Monopoly - circa 1890

These were rich and very enlightened people, yet they were cutthroat competitors operating as entrepreneurs with minimal restrictions. They committed thinly veiled acts of stealing to improve their resources at the expense of their customers and employees. This is the image of the greedy, exploitative capitalist that I want you to have as you consider that just like JAWS, they're b-a-a-a-a-ck!

There are some real bad guys today in corporations but the one, never convicted of any crime, who gets a lot of press for being a modern day Robber Baron is none other than the richest man in the world, William Gates III. Rudolf J. R. Peretz's online book for usinfo.state.gov, full URL shown in sources at end of chapter shows then Microsoft president Bill Gates testifying before the Senate in 1998, at a hearing on anti-competitive issues and technology.

Like Rockefeller before him, Gates was accused of running a monopoly - this time computer software rather than oil. Peretz notes that the distinction between a legitimate, if large, business and an impermissible monopoly is still a work in progress. The picture of Gates captured in his book is shown below in Figure 13-2. A second picture immediately follows.

From Yahoo Answers: *a robber baron is someone that uses unfair tactics for their personal gain they sometimes might use illegal business practices*

> "To some, Bill Gates has become the robber baron of the late 20th century (2) who engages in the classical monopolist behavior that the anti-trust legislation of the United States is specifically designed to prevent. In this view, Microsoft is gouging virtually everyone on the planet through artificially high software prices that it can enforce by intimidating peers and competitors alike.
>
> Bill Gates, well known for his competitiveness, has simply let success go to his head. His fears about non-existent competitive forces have made him paranoid. To protect its dominant position and to maximize revenue and net income, Microsoft is stifling competition and software innovation.
>
> In the robber baron view, the Department of Justice is right on target in its efforts to clip the wings of Microsoft and allow more competition into the world of operating systems and application software."

Figure 13-2 Bill Gates, Modern Robber Baron?

Arthur Anderson was bottom of the rubble pile

During the Bush years, in the early 2000's, companies like Enron (not Exxon), Global Crossings and others made the news for their management's utter disregard for corporate or human ethics as they operated in a corrupt manner motivated by greed and then they lied to protect their gains. These corporate titans were made temporary heroes, but it was not that long that their actions put their companies out of business, creating havoc not just for the rich and the well-to-do but also for small investors whose entire pensions were eliminated.

If today's overly greedy and corrupt corporate citizen's need a face, it's the face of Enron, or Global Crossings, and for good measure, let's throw in the worst face of them all, Arthur "trust-me, I'm an auditor" Anderson.

Bernie Madoff had not even been born yet. OK, he was but he had not yet been discovered by our billion-dollar bank examiners. In the wake of the biggest corporate scandal of all time, in 2008, the banks were about to collapse, GM and Chrysler were about to go under and everybody's pensions made them look like they had chosen not to save for a rainy day. Could corporations have again been the cause?

Going back just a bit in time, but in the same spirit of a thief such as Bernie Madoff, Arthur Anderson, later re-formed as *Accenture,* after its scandal, attested to the falsifications of huge corporate clients such as Enron. Before its demise, Arthur Andersen Consulting swore on a stack of bibles that they did no wrong.

Still other companies such as Adelphia and even Martha Stewart Living found ways to stiff the public of its financial opportunities while they made or hoped to make a killing for themselves. Is Bernie Madoff serving time for all of the thieves in the banking industry? Why is he the only one there? Their greed created major hardships for many people and they too should do time with Bernie. In 2017, they made a movie out of it—*The Wizard of Lies.*

Madoff was sentenced to 150 years in prison. He is paying for his crimes with a sentencing of 150 years in prison, which is actually the maximum amount of years allowed.

Call it "greed." And remember that the famous Philosopher Eric Fromm saw greed as "...a bottomless pit which exhausts the person in an endless effort to satisfy the need without ever reaching satisfaction." Sounds like Fromm had been talking to Twilight Zone's Rod Serling. With men and women of greed instead of creed in positions of trust, running the corporations of America, what better should we expect?

In 2010, we notice a bit of a shift in power. The government has assumed all power, or so it seems. Government greed and the prior Administration's lust for power is endless. Things change immediately after Americans said no to four more years of Obama via Hillary Clinton and already America is on a path of recovery. Big corporations are getting talks out by the woodshed when they behave in an ant-American fashion. Corporations, with a new 21% tax rate have no beef with this president though the end of crony capitalism came with Trump's 2017 inauguration.

Corporations that played ball with the government in the latter part of 2009, were a phenomenal source of capital for the government and its minions -- or better yet, the corporate minions, and the government contracts they controlled. Americans are glad the crony capitalism days are behind us.

Can you imagine all that money that needed to be given to all the cronies? Though corporations have no hands, they were first in line to fill the company coffers with good old green government cash. Considering what really happened, it is highly improbable that the change the young voters were looking for in 2008 ever came. Now, with a president trying to make America great again, millennials don't know what happened. There guy did not deliver and for some reason they don't like the guy who is offering them a better life.

In the corporate world, there is enough money at stake that the notion of "you lie, and I'll swear to it" took root for eight years and was SOP. Consequently, there was always an abundance of liars to go around the corporate boardroom, devising and agreeing to schemes to bilk the unknowing of their hard earned income

And, just like Arthur Anderson, now sunning in a new corporate form in Bermuda as Accenture, there are still enough swearers out there to match the liars. These complicit corporate auditing firms are willing to look the other way or give a customary wink and a nod in order to sustain and grow their own business opportunities. After all, who wants to lose a "client" on a technicality?

Time for a structural change

You don't have to look far anymore to find somebody out there willing to give up integrity in a heart-beat to increase their bank accounts. It is a real shame. Bob Yanelavage, a barber in Plymouth PA, runs his small business on Main Street. By all accounts, Bob thinks that people should be honest and that's that. Yet, Bob is a very smart guy and he knows that we are all hurting partly because our representatives are not honest. They hide under the radar and they are disinterested in the people's business. Corporations exist because dishonorable representatives such as these, say they should!

The whole notion of corporations and the huge tractor trailer loads of cash they handle clearly provides more seedy opportunities than the normal executive or politician can resist. And so, we, who elect those who give corporations their power, reap what we sew. It's time to demand a change. Go ahead and get a haircut at Bob's to make your point.

And, when you go to Bob's shop, make sure you tell him thanks just for being a great American. He is a small businessman who thinks of people first, and profit second. Profit will come if the people see the quality and value in his service. So, why doesn't every politician have to be something else before they become a politician? And, I am sorry, community organizer does not fill the bill as a real job.

Name Some Names

Just as in the original Robber Baron days, we know who the individual perpetrators are since their names are on the indictments. If it were not for indictments, however, these @$%^&%$#@'s would continue to be anonymous, clipping the fabric of the U.S.A. every chance they get and admitting nothing. You know that more are out there to be discovered but they surely are busy covering their tracks.

In this age we have seen names like the late Ken Lay of Enron and Gary Winnick of Global Crossings, both associated with corporate corruption at its max. And, of course the face of corruption in 2009, was Bernie Madoff.

Unless caught, the Lays and Winnick's, and Madoffs, and the new barons, still operating behind the corporate veil, are unrepentant and continually in denial. We should deal with them all by watching them even closer. Until we see a paradigm shift in boardroom ethics, we should not expect any better behavior. Why? Because the stakes are so high and because we know from Eric Fromm that greed is bottomless. But, there is more good news. Donald Trump is watching the game.

Bernie Madoff's clients took a bath and were not bailed out at all. The big rich did not take care of the little rich. The corporate moguls took care of themselves and let the little guys like Bernie's clients take the full rap. AIG and Fannie and Freddie and Citibank and Goldman Sachs initially took a bath but their friends in the Congress of our United States bailed them out. They were too big to fail. Stockholders were bailed out and their executives still got their bonuses while Bernie's people are now washing dishes. Corporations are not fair, but government is less fair.

My friend, the government

In his book, The Truth About the "Robber Barons," author Thomas Di Lorenzo defines a *market entrepreneur* as a capitalist who succeeds financially by selling a newer, better, or less expensive product, on the free market, with no government subsidies, direct or indirect. He must please his customer to get the business since the consumer is the final determinant as to who gets the sale.

He sees a *political entrepreneur* as one who succeeds primarily by influencing government to subsidize his business or industry or to enact legislation or regulation that harms his competitors.

In his book, The Big Rip-off: How Big Business and Big Government Steal Your Money, author Timothy P. Carney dispels the widespread myth that Big Business and Big Government are rivals -- that Big Business wants small government, a "level playing field" and a "bare minimum of regulation."

Carney says, "Not so," and he demonstrates in his book how some big businesses, more than you may think, together with elected officials of both parties, are doing everything possible to replace America's robust free market with a web of government handouts, stricter regulation, higher taxes, and other special favors to stifle competition. The losers: smaller competitors, less established businesses, consumers, employees, and taxpayers. The bottom line losers -- you and me. Did the former Obama administration changed this notion or exacerbated it?

So, the modern Robber Baron, the corporation has a partner in crime, the US government. From our work in prior chapters, we know that the Constitution does not deal specifically with the notion that government and industry would collude against the people. Who would have ever thought that such controls would be necessary?

The Founding Fathers could not conceive that the representatives of the people would sell out the people so regularly. Corporations were not a big part of the landscape in America in the 18th century, and the prevailing thought on the English corporations was disdain and contempt. One could extend, that if there were as many corporations as today, the Founding Fathers would have created a much thicker Constitution and corporations would be subjugated overall to the will of the people. .

America, long the land of the free and the home of the brave and the land of unlimited opportunity under the former president was becoming the land of corporate-only crony-only opportunity.

Without working through conspiracy theories, which I do not subscribe to, the facts show that regular Americans are under attack in our own country on many fronts. Our government for the last eight years, through our representatives, many of questionable character, has chosen to ignore the Constitution that we do have as it passes "illegal" laws that the legislators themselves often choose not to read. With Trump now at the helm, finally normal Americans have a chance.

Lap dog corporations love lap dog representatives and they make a beautiful team. The friendly corporation meets the friendly representative. They take turns opening their wallets to receive their due tribute for services rendered. Corporations always stand ready to gain more power and influence and profit for the ruling class. With the vast resources corporations have, and the more they are given by our lawmakers, the more dangerous it is to be in their crosshairs by design or by accident.

Corporations have no reason to like you as a member of the citizenry, and they don't like you, and they never will. In fact, when they look into the mirror and see a soulless nothing that takes and never gives, they do not even like themselves.

Even the corporate officers get a little sick to their stomachs thinking about their own personal greed and selfishness. Yet, even in melancholy, the corporate titan of yesterday or today is pleased to crush anything that attempts to diminish his opportunity for more profits. If you happen to be in his way, check your healthcare policy if you still have one!

The old-time robber barons

The robber barons in their heyday were involved in lots of big ventures. One such opportunity was the building of the transcontinental railroad. Don't think for a minute that the railroad barons used only their own money. What we know today as corporate welfare was well practiced even in the 19th century. There were those at the time that felt that the free market could not have come up with adequate capital to create the railroad that crossed the entire continent. We should have given it a shot with the railroads.

The Union Pacific and the Central Pacific received subsidies based on each mile of track laid. They received low interest "loans" and big land grants to assure the rights-of-way's. Other large projects however, such as the Great Northern Railroad were financed privately. Thus, the Union Pacific and Central Pacific railroads received welfare from the people and the Great Northern had to do it by itself.

It doesn't seem fair does it? A wise man once said, "It isn't what you know, it's who you know," and those with government connections, the political entrepreneurs always have the edge on the market entrepreneurs when competing for the same markets.

The smell of collusion was rampant in the building of the subsidized railways. For example, there was a lot of politicking but Jay Cooke, an American financier who made a ton in financial markets used so much of his own money in the Northern Pacific Railroad, that he went bankrupt and sold his shares for pennies on the dollar.

He was not too pleased that the Government backed the Union Pacific and Central Pacific as they built the first transcontinental railroad. Wikipedia chronicles the history of the transaction quite well on its site. Congress passed the necessary legislation and subsidies.

With government bailouts, has GM become the new Union Pacific and is Chrysler the Central Pacific? What would that make Ford—an American Car Company?

The railroad construction was planned by Theodore Judah. The Congress gave the OK in 1862 and some independent financing came from other magnates who participated in the building. They were known both as the Big Four and as the Associates. These four were Sacramento, California businessmen Leland Stanford, Collis Huntington, Charles Crocker, and Mark Hopkins. The group entrusted Crocker with the construction mission. Much of the labor was provided by Chinese workers, who like today's illegal foreign nationals, worked for a pittance.

Figure 13-3 Good Old Fashioned Robber Baron Depiction (Web)

Not only did these magnates make out on the deal, so did the politicians. Their perks included things that you don't see unless you pay attention. For example, what looks like a railroad bed for industry may not really be so. The perks included separate rail lines besides those heading cross country. These were required to be built to serve communities represented by influential members of Congress even if those lines were not economical. How about a nice set of tracks right up to the side door of your home?

Railroads and Scranton, PA

There has been rumor in Scranton Pennsylvania (true or not?) for years that the coal baron family of former Governor William Scranton had a caboose or two and an engine ready to go at the drop of a hat on a spur that connected their property to the railroad system. They had this in the event that the coal miners were to strike. Their mini-train would save the family. Noblesse-oblige was not always the order of the day for the wealthy.

The late John Murtha was ready at all times to take off from the infamous John Murtha Airport and there was always a seat in the snack bar, the main concourse, the men's room, and anywhere else that you look. Echoes are also commonplace at the John Murtha International Airport, but there is nobody there anymore to hear them.

The robber barons of the 19th Century had it all and like the corporate billionaires of today basically they could do whatever they wanted. They owned all of the means of production and they had full control over the components of production, material, labor, finished products, and even distribution.

There was nobody to get in their way other than the government. Somehow during this time, the government, instead of monitoring and controlling, were colluding with and subsidizing robber barons, helping them get richer and richer while the poor were getting poorer and poorer. Workers had no voice. There were no really powerful unions. There were no laws to protect workers from abuse or assure their safety or to protect the environment from the waste that industry was producing. But, soon that would change and then, in the Obama era, corporations regained the chutzpah. Now, Donald Trump controls all the chutzpah!

The turn of the century robber barons rewarded their political allies and like a 21st century video game, they tried to destroy their enemies. They were not beyond colluding with the government (our trusted representatives) or their competitors in restraint of trade so long as this aided them in their pursuit of wealth. They had little regard for the consequences of the acquisition of such wealth. They were as greedy as greedy could get and though they helped America achieve great innovations, they did so on the backs of the poor.

As Samuel Clemens noticed, America has the best politicians money can buy.

http://www.informationclearinghouse.info/article3925.htm

The plight of the worker

For the next 100 years after the Declaration of Independence, the United States was largely an agricultural nation. Unskilled workers fared poorly in the early U.S. economy. They received as little as half the pay of skilled craftsmen, artisans, and mechanics. Forty percent or so of the workers in the bigger cities, not involved in agriculture, worked for low wages. They served as general laborers, seamstresses in clothing factories, or other mass production undertakings.

In many ways, other than the general American opportunity, the common worker lived most always in dismal circumstances. With the rise of industrial factories, children, women, and an ever-increasing supply of poor immigrants were commonly employed to run the machines. Is there any question as to why the Illegal immigrant of 2010 is well appreciated by the "barons" of today?

Labor arbitrage -- the lowest wage possible

As industry grew in the late 19th century and the 20th century, many Americans left the farms and small towns to work in these new factories. The factories were organized for mass production, and thus relied heavily on a ready supply of unskilled labor willing to work for the lowest wage possible.

During this period, labor arbitrage, an ugly term at best, was quite prevalent. In the current day and for the past forty years or so, the notion of labor arbitrage again has raised its ugly head as the motivation for off-shoring and outsourcing of jobs to the lowest bidder. Labor arbitrage was operating in the 19th century as the industrialists held all the cards.

The well-known robber barons and later the factory barons in the new industrial age, were so concerned about their business matters that the lowly worker was the last one considered.

The barons were most concerned about the ultimate survivability of their enterprises. However, once they knew they were going concerns, other important things, such as increased profits, and beating the competition at all costs quickly took the top listings on their agendas. If the worker had any place at all on their to-do-lists, it was to convince the worker to provide their service for the smallest amount of pay possible. The story of the Unions role in labor arbitrage is given in detail in Chapter 14.

Though our elected representatives, throughout history, were to be serving the public and not themselves--and not the elite, it was the elite with whom they fraternized, and it was the elite who provided them with perks that they could never achieve being part of the John Q. Public fraternity. So, the thought of taxation without real representation was and continues to be a natural.

The British pulled up stakes long ago and the French left without even saying adieu, yet in the prior president's administration, normal everyday Americans again found themselves facing a world in which we were taxed and taxed and taxed and if there were another day of representation, it would be lonesome.

The citizens suffer from the Congress's preoccupation with the matters of big business and big people and the lack of concern for the voters (We the People), who put them in office. Thankfully, as in the cases of Ken Lay, (Enron), Gary Winnick (Global Crossings), John Rigas (Adelphia), Martha Stewart, and of course Bernie Madoff, the new barons care enough about the American judicial system at least enough to answer their subpoenas.

...

Chapter Summary

The Robber Barons of old and today's corporations acting as the new Robber Barons have too much in common. Using excessive work visas of all flavors, off-shoring, and illegal aliens, today's Robber Barons have figured out how to defeat the unions and the workers at the same time through labor arbitrage.

There are many opinions about how corporations came to have such power. Though nobody appears to be taking action to reduce corporate power, the scholars upon examination of the facts and the fourteenth amendment have been concluding independently that corporations were never intended by the framers of the fourteenth amendment to have gained super human power.

Though corporations may very well self-destruct over time, the time has come to rein them in by bringing our government back to the people and enacting legislation that will eliminate the potential for harm by these too-well-endowed corporations. And, please in the future when a corporation is dying, do not offer it life support. Check its living will as brought forth by the founding fathers. In other words, let it die, and quickly.

Sources:
http://www.ratical.org/corporations/ToPRaP.html
"http://www.mises.org/story/2317
The Truth About the "Robber Barons"
By Thomas J. DiLorenzo Posted on 9/23/2006
http://www.thirdworldtraveler.com/Corporations/KnowEnemy_ITT.html
http://www.rumormillnews.com/cgi-bin/forum.cgi?read=111114
http://query.nytimes.com/gst/fullpage.html?res=9F02EEDE173DF937A25752C1A96F958260&sec=&spon=&pagewanted=all
http://en.wikipedia.org/wiki/Central_Pacific_Railroad

Chapter 14 Unions Meet the Robber Baron Challenge

Power meets countervailing power

Whenever there is a void, there is an opportunity. The labor arbitrage of the late 19th century affected mostly unskilled workers but in reality, all workers. The greed of the robber barons of this era was so self-centered that they wanted to pay not one penny more than the most meager of subsistence. If they could get away with paying less, they would.

In this environment, labor unions sprang up and gradually developed lots of clout. They offered a power of equal magnitude to the power of employer and they made the worker something that management had to consider if they wanted to be able to run their plants and factories successfully.

The general policy of early labor and trade unions was to rely on discussion and cooperation to secure good working conditions and wages for the workers, but the biggest weapon was the strike and the threat of a strike. Later unions relied on arbitration and education as well as the legislature. At their meetings for example, they would pass resolutions to be brought to the representatives in the hope that legislation would be passed to solve some of the corporate abuses.

As an example of abuse, the work day in the beginning of the 19th century was 12 hours or more and often seven days a week. For all those hours the worker got just enough pay and sometimes not enough pay for a family to make ends meet. It is generally accepted historically that small, local labor unions had been scattered around the thirteen states for about a hundred years before the corporate abuses of the robber barons brought them into the limelight.

The early groups were mostly trade unions in which craftsmen joined together in guilds. The national labor movement in the U.S., however, did not really hit high gear until after the Civil War. The National Labor Union and the Knights of Labor were formed right after the war. The former did not last long (1873), but the Knights of Labor was a viable Union until the 1890's and it did not formally collapse until 1917.

The rise of powerful labor unions

By 1886, the Knights of Labor was losing its prestige for a number of reasons, such as union repression as well as the Knights having lost some key contract negotiations with the railways. Samuel Gompers was quick to step in to fill the void. He founded the American Federation of Labor (AFL) and he served as its first president until his death in 1924.

Prior to the AFL, Gompers had been a local and national labor leader, and with the AFL, he hoped to build the labor movement into a force powerful enough to transform the economic, social and political status of America's workers to more favorable conditions. Gompers was well on his way to achieving his goals for at the time of his death there were over 3 million members of the AFL. It was a very, very powerful union.

As a labor leader, Gompers learned that economic reform was longer lasting than political reform so unlike other leaders, with the AFL, he was not as concerned about getting legislation passed. Gompers had in fact used political clout in one instance in which he had two laws passed regulating what was called the tenement production of cigars.

This law forbade workers in residences to make cigars. Obviously, the Union wanted them to be organized. When Gompers saw that he could get crafty legislation passed but the Supreme Court could just as simply overthrow the law, he began to focus his energies on gaining economic benefits through negotiations and contracts. He learned that which the state may give, the state can also take away but the benefits gained by contract are long lasting. Gompers was no pushover. One of the first acts, for example when he became the president of the AFL was to promote a general strike on May 1, 1886. Its mission was to support an eight-hour workday.

Figure 14-1 Samuel Gompers, President, AFL

Strikes often turned violent

Though he was respected by the captains of industry, nobody made Gompers' life easy. After May 1, 1886, for example, there were still companies insisting on more than 8 hours per day and Gompers insisted that all AFL workers not yet on an 8-hour schedule, were to cease work in a nation-wide strike until their employer would meet the demand. There was a mix of employers who met the demand and those that did not.

Haymarket Riot

There were strike actions all across the country. This was the first national strike ever called. 80,000 marched in Chicago alone and it was seen as the start of a possible revolution. It was taken quite seriously. On May 3, in Chicago, for example, there was a violent confrontation with police. On May 4, a labor meeting was called at a location called Haymarket to discuss the brute force of the activities the day before. History notes the meeting was not well planned or organized and the leaders were looking for speakers even as the meeting began.

Then about 100 Chicago police showed up to put down the meeting and have the crowd disburse. When the police showed up, a person, unknown to this day, threw a bomb among the police and chaos erupted.

Nobody could see with the smoke of the bomb in the air and the police panicked. They drew their weapons and began to fire on the crowd. Several in the crowd were killed including a number of policemen. Only one policeman was killed by the bomb and the other dead police were presumed to have been killed by other police firing haphazardly. This event historically is known as the Haymarket Riot and like all good stories there are myths about this event floating around in Chicago to this day.

Rise of the AFL

By 1900, the AFL was booming with memberships and it was soaring faster than any other period in the US labor movement. The "robber barons," a.k.a. "captains of industry," however with their newly formed corporations, did not take too kindly to this decrease in control from accommodating Gompers and his union.

They were not accustomed to sharing power with anybody or anything. To combat the anti-union hostility of the employers, Gompers and the AFL were eventually forced to go back to a political strategy to seek protective legislation from angry employers who were, to say the least, not very nice.

Corporations strike back

Never punch a man with two-fists ready to go. To retaliate for their own losses, companies had begun to sue the unions using the same anti-trust laws that had been passed to weaken those very companies. Workers began to fear that actions could come back to bite them if each member were to be found liable for treble damages from the strikes and boycotts that they were so effectively waging. Of course, there were many corrupt judges in the hip-pockets of well moneyed corporatists.

The Union's new friend - the elected

So, guess who the unions had to become buddies with? Your friendly congressional representatives. In fact, the unions put forth union-friendly candidates for the very purpose of affecting their legislation. Considering that most of the voters were workers and not employers, it is not too hard to imagine that the union candidates at this time in history, with unions being so popular, had no trouble getting elected. Unions were in America to stay and they would never be less than a major force with which to be reckoned.

The CIO

Gompers' A.F. of L as it was called, had been mostly a craft union that had little to do with unskilled labor. Some think this had a lot to do with race as skilled workers were mostly white. Regardless of the rationale, the American Federation of Labor was reluctant to organize unskilled workers.

Every void is an opportunity for someone. This someone was John L. Lewis, known for his work with the Mining Unions in the mid 1900's. Lewis created the Committee for Industrial Organization within the A.F. of L. in 1935. The A.F. of L. did not really like this and so Lewis took these unions in 1938, and he created a new organization called the Congress of Industrial Organizations. Thus, the A.F. of L. and C.I.O. had separate existences until an agreement was effected in 1955, which created what we now know as the AFL-CIO.

Labor Organizers like Samuel Gompers and John L. Lewis were brave and gutsy and in many ways arrogant. They had to be all of that to stand up to the powerful robber barons of the day. John L. Lewis for example pulled a power play on the strength of his Union affiliation back in 1940. He was a Republican, which was very unusual for a union man. Nonetheless, he had backed Roosevelt for several elections.

For his own reasons, he wanted Roosevelt out of the White House. So, he made a vow with the American people that if Franklin Roosevelt was elected president again, he would resign from his presidency of the C.I.O. The power-play did not work. Roosevelt was elected and, Lewis kept his word, and the C.I.O. Presidency passed to Philip Murray, who had been President of the United Steel Workers.

Figure 14-2 John L. Lewis C.I.O.

When Murray died in 1952, Walter Reuther, whose background was the United Auto Workers became the last president of the C.I.O before its merger with the A.F. of L. Clearly the AFL-CIO is the largest labor Union in America today at 13 million members.

One of its fastest growing affiliates is the 1.4 million strong American Federation of State, County and Municipal Employees (AFSCME). Recognizing the importance of political affiliation, AFSCME hopes to be able to influence your representative for U.S. President and the Union went on record in 2008 to endorse Hillary Clinton for President.

However, when Hillary Clinton did not win her first attempt at a presidential nomination in June 2008, the AFL-CIO endorsed Barack Obama and worked hard for his election. In support of the candidate Obama, the AFL-CIO launched a new website: Meet Barack Obama.

In its endorsement statement, the General Board of the union noted that Sen. Barack Obama "has secured the nomination of his party in a campaign that has energized millions of Americans and spoken to the hopes and dreams of people from every corner of our nation."

The Web site continued: "His leadership can re-engage disenfranchised Americans and bring our country together. Sen. Obama has advocated a change of direction for our nation that mirrors the priorities of the labor movement."

Democrats looking back find it embarrassing and tough to admit that they got little of what they expected from former President Obama in his eight years. The irony is that Obama was more of a Wall-Street and corporate guy and if the truth be known, he enjoyed being the CEO of GM and Chrysler and Solyndra all at the same time.

Ironically, organized labor had high hopes for Senator Barack Obama before he became president. Labor, in 2008, had contributed a reported $400 million to the Democratic Party and naturally expected, quid pro quo, hoping to get something meaningful in return.

Organized labor honestly thought this exciting, liberal hipster from Chicago was the answer to all their prayers. But unfortunately for the unions, our former president, the man who said, "Politics didn't lead me to working folks; working folks led me to politics," did not do too much to help working folks.

He freely acknowledged the importance and the legitimacy of organized labor. Nonetheless while having control of the situation, he never really showed a genuine belief in the righteousness of the labor movement, from labor's perspective. He did not, in labor's view, demonstrate a belief in the moral primacy of working people. In retrospect, liberal authors suggest that the only thing Obama demonstrated for labor was that he could not be trusted. Many would add that it was more than labor that had that feeling.

One of Obama's big failings with labor was the EFCA (Employee Free Choice Act), for instance. This would have given workers the right to join a union without having to navigate the treacherous waters of management hate-campaigns or long, drawn-out NLRB elections. If the EFCA was in effect in the fashion prescribed by big labor, workers could join a union simply by signing cards ("card check"). If a majority said they wished to belong to a union, presto! — they were union members — which is more or less how they do it in Europe and Canada. Only in these United States is joining a union nearly as complicated as becoming a citizen.

While the former president did acknowledge his nominal support of EFCA, he did it flatly, mechanically, coming off more like an accountant than a champion of the labor cause. He bunted instead of hitting a home run with the issue. Instead of going on national television and presenting the EFCA inspirationally insisting that the country could not do without the legislation as a monument to worker empowerment, Obama instead turned the job over to chief of staff Rahm Emanuel and more or less bowed out of the scenario.

And, so, Emanuel, a pure politician began giving Republicans concessions to the point that the bill if passed would no longer have achieved labor's goals. As expected, with the former president conspicuously silent, and no one to lead the charge, the legislation, even in its weakened, watered-down form, died a natural death. This was not labor's only disappointment with Barack Obama.

Ironically, conservatives hated Obama with good reason but he was so duplicitous on many issues that even those who would have been friends were simply never sure.

Answering the opportunity

To answer the opportunity that arose when America's mostly unskilled laborers were subjected to starving wages, local unions formed to help pressure the ruling class into providing a better work environment. Over time, big national unions took over most of the small unions and today we find the AFL-CIO, and the Teamsters as two of the largest unions in the U. S. A.

Unions provide a very important countervailing force against the power of the corporations who in many cases have colluded with government officials to gain advantages. There are very few companies today who like IBM in the 1970's and 1980's put the employee first and expect the employee to do their best for the company.

In the Obama era, corporate greed was everywhere but for his own reasons, Obama was not such a great friend to labor. He was more into crony capitalism. Now, with Donald Trump being a people president, corporations have toned down and crony capitalism is not as prevalent.

The ruling class does not want to pay any more than the minimum and the workers want enough for subsistence and a level of enjoyment. Traditionally, since they gained power in the 1890s, unions have provided this for employees and this is why employees faithfully pay their union dues.

Offshoring & illegal immigration

The notions of offshoring and illegal immigration have posed big problems for unions, none of which it seems the unions have been able to solve. Offshoring as it is known today for professional jobs is not a loss for the unions since most professionals work directly for their companies with no union protection.

The fact is that a worker has no employment rights at work unless he or she is part of a collective bargaining agreement. Why Unions are not making hay on this is a big question and for workers paying dues, it should be a big concern.

Labor Unions again are also doing poorly in terms of being a countervailing force for illegal immigrants taking U.S. jobs. Despite these shortcomings, organized labor is still a very important political and economic force today, but its influence has waned markedly.

Manufacturing, where unions once thrived has declined substantially, and the service sector has grown. Unskilled blue collar jobs are not as abundant as in the early 1990's. Unions have become very powerful in education and government under AFSCME and this is one of their major strongholds today. Overall the # of unionized workers in the US declines every year.

With Donald Trump bringing in jobs, jobs, and more jobs, and corporations are seemingly treating employees better, the idea of a compelling reason for unions is in question. We'll see.

Sources:

http://www.aflcio.org/aboutus/history/history/gompers.cfm
http://www.kentlaw.edu/ilhs/haymkmon.htm
http://www.freerepublic.com/focus/f-news/1755355/posts
http://www.lawyersandsettlements.com/articles/01056/illegal_immigrant_crackdown.html
http://www.fraudfactor.com/ffunionfraudintro.html
http://www.commondreams.org/headlines/021700-02.htm

Chapter 15 Worker Visas Take Many American Jobs

Onshore vs. offshore

The big difference between losing your job to a person with an H-1B Visa and having your job offshored is whether the person who gets your job will be playing a home game or an away game. If they get to work in their own country, say India for example, then for them it is a home game. Your job has been offshored.

If instead, they get an H-1B Visa, then they get to come to the U.S. to take your job. In the latter scenario, however, your company or the company that would have hired you first lies about your availability to work or they would not get the H-1B visa slot. The next lie is that they will pay the H-1B visa worker or any other work visa, the same pay for the same work that you would have done. But, of course, it is all a lie

Visa alphabet soup

We can always thank the Greeks for the alphabet, because overall, the U.S. visa problem is not stuck on the letters H-1B. There are several visa types for just about as many letters fashioned for us by the Greeks and Phoenicians many, many years ago. As you would expect, in addition to H-1B, there is an H-1A, and there are visa types that start with A and go to T with many variants within those letters.

Right now, there are 81 different visa types, each promising somebody in the world the opportunity to come to the U.S. for one reason or another. In prior versions of this book, I displayed a reworked a table from a government site, If you would like to see the current table, rather than type the four line URL, just type *Immigration Classifications and Visa Categories* into your browser and you can see the full chart, and all of its meaning as well as other information that you may find interesting on the topic.

Actually, there are so many visa types that foreigners interested in coming to the U.S. often use one type of visa that they can get rather than the type of visa that they actually should get for the type of work or study that they are hoping to do. It is a bureaucratic nightmare that only a desperate non-citizen or a lawyer could be paid enough to want to fully understand. That's why the latter make a lot of money on the former trying to squeeze them in.

With Trump in control of the whole US bureaucracy today, one would hope that he can find a few conservatives to rework the whole visa system to assure that it serves America and Americans rather than foreigners and the politicos who enriched themselves by designing such a poor system for our nation.

H-1B and white collar tech workers

All of the visa programs have the opportunity for abuse, but none has come under as much fire as the H-1B Visa program. This is the first time I can recall that the government has invited foreigners to take the jobs of Americans. Displaced white-collar workers from this visa program and from offshoring have been creating quite a stir about their government's acceptance of the job losses suffered by American citizens.

Corporations, who we know from the last several chapters cannot be trusted, lobby that they need H-1B visas to compete in the world market (meaning they want to pay lower wages). Just like George Bush says illegal aliens do work that Americans won't do, corporations say there are not enough American workers to fill their high-tech jobs. It's all bunk. It's all labor arbitrage at its best.

Millennials have it the worst, but generation Z will not be much better in terms of earning a good wage with all of the visa holders in the US> DRUC-H1-B. Democrats and Republicans in Congress both hoodwinked the millennials by their unholy alliance on H1-B visas to import millions of cheap indentured servants. Millennial's colleges stiffed them also by never making them take Econ 101, where they would learn about supply and demand: If the government brings in millions of cheap foreign workers to pay back tech companies for their contributions, millennials cannot get a good salary. Some think that 70-100K is good because their English major buddies are not making that, but, in reality 70-100K was the going wage for techs in 90's. If it was not for visas such as H1-B, millennials would be making 150K right out of school. No kidding.

There are about 300,000 high tech students that graduate from American Universities each year and yet there are only about 120,000 jobs for them to get. So, who is lying, the corporations or the statistics? I think we know. Why should the few jobs we produce go to illegal foreign nationals?

The fact is corporations do not want to find Americans for jobs when legal or illegal foreign nationals will work for so much less. For this alone, all Congressmen should not regain their offices when they run next time. Fire them unless they are willing to work for severely reduced wages and no expenses.

Congress is simply corrupt. It has permitted law firms to get around the intent of U.S. law which is to hire American's first if available. These firms have not only figured out ways for companies to prove that Americans will never be available, one firm was so bold as to explain their scheme on YouTube. Use your search engine next chance you have, and type in YouTube H-1B and see what you get. On June 21, 2007, Computerworld did an expose on this scam. It has not gotten any better. Here is an excerpt from that article:

> June 21, 2007 (Computerworld) -- WASHINGTON -- That explosive H-1B YouTube video offering advice on how to hire foreign workers instead of Americans has gotten the attention of U.S. Sen. Charles Grassley, (R-Iowa), and Rep. Lamar Smith, (R-Texas), who called it evidence of abuse of the visa program. Both men want a federal investigation and are seeking answers from the law firm that posted the original video on YouTube.
>
> In a letter to U.S. Department of Labor Secretary Elaine Chao, Grassley and Smith characterized the video as "exposing the

blatant disregard for American workers and the deliberate attempt to bring in cheaper foreign workers through the H-1B program." They also ... want the labor secretary to review the video and investigate "the law firm's unethical procedures and advice to clients."

In the video, a person identified as Lawrence Lebowitz, an attorney at the firm Cohen & Grigsby PC in Pittsburgh, explains how U.S. companies can avoid hiring U.S. workers. "Our goal is clearly not to find a qualified and interested U.S. worker," said Lebowitz in the video. "And that, in a sense, sounds funny, but it's what we are trying to do here."

Other companies help steal American's jobs

If an IT worker tries to get a job with one of the companies that like to spoof the system, the company, of course does not expect that the IT worker will complain because individuals do not have as many lawyers as any company does to figure out what is what.

You see, if you are available to work and the employer of the person who gets the job ignores that fact and they hire someone from Bhopal or Japan instead, for example, they are not operating within the U.S. Law.

But they are corporations and you are powerless against them.

They simply do not care about normal people because their lawyers will solve everything for them. Smart lawyers know how to get a good deal for their clients, and though you may wind up unfairly on the wrong side of the deal, the lawyers will sanitize it for the company so that it is as easy as clicking on Murthy's Web site. http://www.murthy.com/h1bvisa.html

Here's a little bit of what they would find from the above click:

> What We Can Do For You : At the Murthy Law Firm, we can consult with you to determine that the nature of the position and the beneficiary's background are appropriate for the H-1B, and suggest alternatives if the initial proposal is not a viable option. We can advise both the employer and prospective employee

regarding the H-1B documentation requirements and legal issues. We can also prepare paperwork and submit it to the Department of Labor and USCIS.

That beneficiary they are talking about is the guy from Bhopal. By the way, it helps in this light to know what a beneficiary actually is. I picked the definition that seems to me to best apply to the situation at hand. A beneficiary is:

> A person or entity who is the recipient of or will receive some or all proceeds of money or property held by the current owner upon a specified event or condition.

Trade agreements negotiated by buffoons

Many remember the big hoopla with NAFTA and GATT. President Bill Clinton, Hillary's husband at the time, took many bows for completing these treaties. Guess what? Our negotiators locked in the minimum # of H-1B visas at 65,000 in exchange for the passage of the trade agreements. That means every year at least 65,000 new high-tech workers from India or South Africa or some other location come to the U.S. and Congress's great trade negotiators took away our power to shut off the spigot.

With the six-year option, that is 390,000 new high-tech jobs taken by legal foreign nationals every six years. If you think that after six years, they will really go home, think again as—they will never go home! Don't you just love our corrupt Congress.

Now, because the Obama government saved money by not sending its negotiators to negotiating school, Congress no longer has the option under the agreements to ever reduce that number without violating the trade agreements. This is just another example of our friendly representatives working on behalf of special interests and corporations and not the people.

Again, there is a Clinton in the foray. This time it was Hillary, who must have believed that these middle-class voters were all Republicans as she pushed hard in favor of corporations over the entire U.S. middle class. Lou Dobbs called it like it is: "Clinton is "selling out our middle class on H-1B visas." Taxation but no representation is what we have been experiencing for a long time. A mistake maybe, but a mistake that helps the ruling class and not the college graduate who just lost her opportunity for the American dream.

Trump to the rescue

In two of his first acts as president of the United States, just days after his inauguration in 2017, Donald Trump formally withdrew the United States from the ill-conceived Trans-Pacific Partnership, and he served notice to Mexico and Canada that he would seek to renegotiate the North American Free Trade Agreement (NAFTA) to get a better deal for American workers. He was absolutely right to do so. Finally, there is a US president who really wants to make America great again.

Chapter Summary

There are over 80 visa types. Only foreign nationals and corporate lawyers understand them all. They are the means that people from other countries use to get an extended stay in the United States and if they decide to go on a booze bender for a few months, the US welfare system will bail them out.

Many of the visa types permit the workers to have gainful employment in the United States. Others, such as the L1, H-1B, O1, etc. actually are the ticket for gainful employment and a reasonably long-time-period for U.S. temporary residency.

Visas are good for the U.S. in many ways. Unfortunately, opportunistic corporations and law firms have found a way to reduce company expenses by bringing workers in under these visas to replace higher-priced American workers. Often the citizen must train the foreign national to do his or her job before they are out of work. Yes, our Congress did this to us.

Congress has been lobbied profusely by the rich ruling class, especially Bill Gates of Microsoft, to do away with the visa caps (now back to 65,000 from over 200,000 in 2004) completely. Gates seems to be convinced that Americans either are not smart enough or want too much money. I'm thinking the latter.

Gates suggests that business will be crippled if it must be limited to hiring Americans or permitting them to keep their jobs when foreign nationals who are either smarter or who will work for less can be available almost immediately

It's time to outsource guys like Bill Gates and other corporate titans and their henchmen in management to a country that will accept them. Then, we can go back to being an America for Americans.

Additionally, there may be 435 representatives and 100 senators available for the trip overseas after the next election for the outsourcing pool if we are smart enough to do what is right. Throw the bums out!

Recent update and perspective on trade

This piece is excellent. Buffoons negotiate for the US.

Free trade in an Unfree Trade World is Economic Suicide For the USA
Raymond Richman, 7/23/2015
http://www.idealtaxes.com/post3896.shtml

> George Washington in his farewell address urged the US to "Avoid foreign entanglements." How right he was. US foreign entanglements began with a vengeance under Presidents Wilson and Franklin D Roosevelt—especially the latter. The Bretton Woods agreements which were negotiated by Harry Dexter White, as the U.S. representative, later exposed as a Communist spy, created the World Bank and the International Monetary Fund.
>
> Benn Steil, senior fellow and director of international economics at the Council on Foreign Relations in New York, founding editor of International Finance, a top scholarly economics journal, in his book, *The Battle of Bretton Woods: John Maynard Keynes, Harry Dexter White,*

and the Making of a New World Order (Council on Foreign Relations, (Princeton University Press, 2013), discussing the creation at Bretton Woods of the World Bank and the IMF writes.

Together with the United Nations, they marked the beginning of Post WWII's march toward global government and simultaneously the march toward state capitalism, a political mixture of a powerful state, socialist enterprises, and state-dominated private capitalist enterprises.

Mussolini, a former Communist, and Hitler, a national socialist were the first world leaders to recognize the power of the new economic system. Both freed themselves from the ideology of Marxism and both recognized how a socialist state could dominate private enterprises and bend their will to the service of the state.

New Deal innovations included the minimum wage and the Davis-Bacon Act, two laws to advantage labor unions, which returned blacks to conditions worse than slavery by denying Blacks equal opportunities for employment since the unions at that time were nearly all lily-white.

...

The USA continues with its foolish trade policies, the latest being the fast-track Trade Promotion Authority requested by Pres. Obama. It is ludicrous to read the U.S. Chamber of Commerce pamphlet entitled "America Needs Trade Promotion Authority". It points out correctly that U.S. exports provide job opportunities for American workers but make no mention of the fact that increased imports, and the trade deficits, cause a net loss of millions of jobs.

The trade agreements not only have created trade deficits for the U.S. but encouraged American manufacturers to move production of their products abroad. Economists Justin R. Pierce, on the staff of the Federal Reserve Board, and Yale professor of economics Peter K. Schott wrote in 2012 that one result of the U.S.-China trade agreement of 2000 was a sharp drop in U.S. manufacturing employment after 2001 resulting from the elimination of trade policy uncertainty. As a result American companies produced their products abroad and exported them to the U.S. free of duty. The list of companies that moved their production overseas reads like a Who's Who in the US Chamber of Commerce.

--End of post--

Two comments on this partial post are also right on the mark. They are shown below. Enjoy!

Comment by M, 7/25/2015:

Boy, the way Glen Miller played.
Songs that made the hit parade.

Guys like us, we had it made.
Those were the days.
Didn't need no welfare state.
Everybody pulled his weight.
Gee, our old LaSalle ran great.

Those were the days.

And you know who you were then.
Girls were girls and men were men.
Mister, we could use a man like Herbert Hoover again.
People seemed to be content.Fifty dollars paid the rent.
Freaks were in a circus tent.

Those were the days.

Take a little Sunday spin. Go to watch the Dodgers win.
Have yourself a dandy day that cost you under a fin!
Hair was short and skirts were long.
Kate Smith really sold a song.
I don't know just what went wrong.

Those Were The Days!!!!!!!

Comment by Ray Tapajna, 1/23/2016:

Excellent article - However, even talking about our present day free trade as trade has to change. Free trade is not trade as historically practiced and defined. It is more about dividing investments from production and moving production anywhere in the world for the sake of cheaper labor for the sake of investments. It does not work. Our economies based on making money on money instead of making things are burning out across the world.

President Clinton had to bail out the process in 1995 after more than 4000 US factories were moved to Mexico. He had to rush billions of dollars to Mexico to save the value of the peso and the Mexican economy. It was threatening international money values. So the first bail out went to a foreign nation and predicted the coming of the super bail out in 2008 by President Obama. However, he only propped up the big money interests and not anything real. The value of workers and labor is a real money standard and must be in parity with the value of interests or everything will remain economically upside down. Presently, our economy is set in quick sand.
http://tapsearchnews.filetap.com

Sources
http://www.idealtaxes.com/post3896.shtml
http://www.h1b.info/about.php
http://ei.cs.vt.edu/~history/Gates.Mirick.html#family

Chapter 17 Throw the Bums Out Now!

Big problems need big solutions

I began this book by noting the big issues which Americans are facing in this first decade of the 21st Century. Before the big Trump Tax relief of December 2017, which the pundits swear is bogus, keeping income was on the top burner.

There are many other issues. Besides war and peace, even with tax relief, the citizens face huge tax bills, an unresponsive democracy, corporate excess, loss of jobs from visas, offshoring, and illegal aliens, and an election system that needs to be repaired.

These issues affect every American in a big way. Worse than the problems themselves for years, was the fact that no help is on the horizon. The white hat guys were not around the corner. Our representatives were AWOL, but taxation always made the muster. The former president was playing on the other team, and the judiciary began to believe that we the people do not exist. We really love Trump as president for hope now is not just a campaign slogan. Help is now not only around the corner but much of what we need has begun to reach us. What a difference a president makes.

The citizen taxpayers of the U.S. for years have been angry about a lot of things. The list started with corporations pushing down the average wage to subsistence levels, jobs being taken at home and abroad by foreigners with labor unions standing idly by. How about illegal aliens crowding the cities and taking jobs; elections that appear to be rigged, and representatives that do everything but represent the people. Is that enough to make a fella or a gal irate?

The citizen taxpayers of this country are fed up. Yes, we are certainly angry; and our warpath approach to politics was to get Trump elected. Now we have to get some honest men and women into Congress.

Americans are not ready to give it up to anybody now that we have a president working for us. You may remember as a little kid, one day you weren't going to take it any more from the school bully and in exasperation, you finally gave the bully a big push and said, "Come on... you want a piece of me."

One thing is for sure. It is changing but still Democrats and some Republicans have not gotten the country's message. "Represent us or else!" Every politician in every election season from now on better thing action over rhetoric.

The areas in which we presented problems and general solutions in this book, along with a few others that are prevalent are as follows:

- Representation Democracy & Honorable Congressman
- Taxes, Taxes, Taxes
- Fight for Liberty & Representation
- Forming of American Government
- Corporate Power, Greed, & Corruption
- Robber Barons - Old & New
- Countervailing Power - Labor Unions
- Labor Arbitrage --- H-1 B Visas and Other Visas
- Labor Arbitrage --- Offshoring
- Illegal Immigrants

Let's think about these points again so that we can keep coming up with innovative solutions to help make America, great again. There are certainly enough points above that if we were able to effect a solution to them all or a good part of them, we would be well on our way to solving most of the ills of our country. Taxation Without Representation is a problem itself and its only solution is to stop all taxation or to assure honest representation. Let's do both as well as we can.

In no way does the focus on the above points minimize the other issues that need solutions. There are enough topics to be examined in total to create a number of other thick books, to help us be aware and find solutions to the important things we all need to fight to keep America free.

Representation, democracy & honorable congressmen

We always have the choice to take action or do nothing. From ancient times to modern times, good advice suggests that we not sit idly by and let things crush around us. The words of Plato, President James Garfield, the infamous and the insidious Joseph Goebbels, J. Edgar Hoover, and Thomas Jefferson give appropriate caution to sitting idly by or believing that all is OK when it is not:

> "The penalty good men and women pay for indifference to public affairs is to be ruled by evil men." Plato

> "Now more than ever before, the people are responsible for the character of their Congress. If that body be ignorant, reckless, and corrupt, it is because the people tolerate ignorance, recklessness, and corruption. If it be intelligent, brave, and pure, it is because the people demand these high qualities to represent them in the national legislature." James Garfield

> "The great masses of people will more easily fall victims to a 'Big Lie' than a small one, if it is repeated often enough."
> Joseph Goebbels

> "No matter how paranoid or conspiracy-minded you are, what the government is actually doing is worse than you imagine."
> J. Edgar Hoover

> "To consider the judges as the ultimate arbiters of all constitutional questions is a very dangerous doctrine indeed, and on which would place us under the despotism of an oligarchy. Our judges are as honest as other men, and not more so. They have, with others, the same passions for party, for power, and the privilege of their corps.

> ... The constitution has erected no such single tribunal, knowing that to whatever hands confided, with the corruption of time and party, its members would become despots." - 1820 Thomas Jefferson

Is anybody listening?

Sometimes it seems that nobody in government is listening to the people. Of all the topics of the day, especially those that we discuss in this book, our representatives operate their own agendas and do their own will and don't even seem to hear the people. Is our voice being heard but it is being ignored? The Obamacare debacle of 2009 and 2010 is the most flagrant example of this phenomenon. As bad as Obamacare is, the Republican Party in 2017 opted to leave it out there as a memorial to how bad Obama politics were. But, they could have made the politics better and that would have been much better.

Thomas Sowell, one of America's greatest writer was recently quoted as saying that bipartisanism is when Congress from both sides of the aisle get together and they do it doubly wrong. Both parties are mirrors of themselves on the issues.

The only one on the other side is "We-the-People." The thinking of the Democrats in Congress and the former president's and even the Republicans under the Bush Administration was so unified that it reminds me of one of the great sayings attributed to General George S. Patton:

> **When everybody is thinking the same thing; somebody is not thinking!**

Worse than that fact, consider that if there were another good thought in the chambers of the federal government... it would surely be lonesome. Democrats and Republicans are not supposed to be unified. Congress is not supposed to be unified with the President or the Supreme Court. We have separation of powers. A Democratic Congress is supposed to counter the Republican or Democratic president on matters of public importance such as the problem list above, rather than making political statements in the hallowed chambers. So also for a Republican Congress.

Where are the laws to protect the people? Where are the border fences and increased patrols? Where are the congressional voices screaming bloody murder that their constituent's jobs are going overseas? Who is helping millennials? Who is attempting to get student debt canceled or provide a cost of living equalizer rather than penalizing seniors for inflation?

Where are the unions to protect the people from illegal immigrants and corporations? Thank God the Supreme Court is still grumpy and disagreeable or there would be no countervailing power at all. It is like Gary Cooper as John Doe vs. the United Aristocracy? Congress surely can do better and if it won't we must throw them out!

Chapter 18 General Solutions for the Future of the USA

Solutions to crisis of confidence in US government

We have a crisis of confidence in our representative democracy today and so far, at least, nothing is being done to address it. I have five general solutions that I think would help our current legislators, judges, and the President in remembering that their prime mission is to represent the people as they execute their duties. The big problem in terms we all understand is Taxation Without Representation. For your edification and consideration, here is the first General Solution. It is not the product of in-the-box thinking so keep an open mind. The others follow:

General Solution 1: renew oath of office

The gentle and polite way to solve this is to start by simply bringing the Supreme Court Justices into an extended joint session of Congress, with the president in attendance. The Justices would have a big job. Their role would be to swear-in each Senator and each Representative and the president, one more time. The symbolism would be hard not to catch.

This would be a vow renewal just like those who hit a 25th anniversary and they renew their vows, or perhaps a couple who have not been true to each other find a preacher and they decide to recant their old ways and renew the vows they have broken.

Let's bring the Congress and the president into chambers and with C-Span cameras rolling and have them humbly and individually renew their oaths of office. Let their vow renewal make up for the clear trail of broken promises and lack of representation leading back to their swearing-in.

The president should renew his oath first. Followed by each and every congressman. Let each hear the other be sworn in individually, not as a group. Let their voices be recorded forever for posterity. And let's bring them in a few times as a matter of course during their terms - at least every six months so they cannot forget their oaths.

For the second and third and fourth swearing-in during the same term, there shall be no Inaugural Balls required. The tape of each individual oath, all 536 of them, including the VEEP, can be uploaded to YouTube for all the citizens to enjoy. It should be playing softly as background in the government buildings of Washington until we the people think they "get it."

My dad always had this little phrase to pipe back with when asked for something he was not willing to give up. It might be the simple request of a dime for the candy store or it could be one of his friends trying to borrow money. He'd say, "Try and Get it!" I don't think in a thousand Sundays we could get the Congress, president, or Supreme Court to retake their oaths. But, they should.

It would have an impact if we could. So, General Solution # 1, admittedly may never work. If the solution itself does not work, the follow-up to the solution may not work either but let's talk about it as it too has merit in an honest world.

How about a second Joint Session under the auspices of General Solution #1, again with the president and the SCOTUS present. Starting with the president, each one would be asked to take just five minutes to describe how they broke or did not break their oaths (no criminal charges for anything confessed.) since the last oath.

In this five minutes they should also discuss what they will change if they think change is needed regarding their behavior in order to better perform the people's will. The President can take fifteen minutes if needed for all his confessions. Confession is good for the soul and this public confession would be good for America.

Tell me the truth now, wouldn't that be a good restart if only? Take a look at these oaths of office and ask yourself if this has happened.

President's Oath of Office

> "I do solemnly swear (or affirm) that I will faithfully execute the office of President of the United States, and will to the best of my ability, preserve, protect and defend the Constitution of the United States."

Congress - Oath of Office:

> "I do solemnly swear (or affirm) that I will support and defend the Constitution of the United States against all enemies, foreign and domestic; that I will bear true faith and allegiance to the same; that I take this obligation freely, without any mental reservation or purpose of evasion; and that I will well and faithfully discharge the duties of the office on which I am about to enter: So help me God."

The Constitution is quite a document so what we need in the oath is well covered in the Constitution. It certainly would not be bad to have a well-respected religious cleric such as Anne Graham Lotz or Franklin Graham, children of the renowned Dr. Billy Graham add a few points of humility into the oath. Either could make it clear in the swearing-inn speech that our representatives represent the people and not themselves or other interests.

In his book, Civil Disobedience, Henry David Thoreau, the great American author and tax resister, made his own recommendations to improve his government of the 19th century. He called for improving rather than abolishing government:

> "I ask for, not at once no government, but at once a better government..."

Can't we ask for it? Will they submit to the oath renewals or the speech? I surely do not think so. Nonetheless if they did submit, it certainly would be symbolic of a nation trying to heal itself by having the very perpetrators of the problem, the elected politicians, promise they won't be bad anymore. I think it would be a good start.

Since we do not live in Utopia, I do not expect it, but I think it would be good if we were to collectively and singularly ask our representatives to retake their oaths.

Unless they are ready to lie right away, it might give us at least a few good years in which to operate to make the laws catch up with the times, so that we do not have to depend on the good will of hizzoner. And, by the way, while they are at it, during the swearing in, the Chief Justice should announce that herewith the Congress and President are not to be referred to in etiquette as "Your Honor." And, not to be left out, the Chief Justices should renew their oaths at the same time"

Supreme Court Justice Oath of Office

> "I, [NAME], do solemnly swear (or affirm) that I will administer justice without respect to persons, and do equal right to the poor and to the rich, and that I will faithfully and impartially discharge and perform all the duties incumbent upon me as [TITLE] under the Constitution and laws of the United States. So help me God."

And for good measure it wouldn't be a bad idea to bring the names of the Supreme Court Justice's to the people once every six years during election time. If the people approve, the justice's get six more years before they need re-approval. If the people disapprove, the justices who are not approved are sent home with the election losers. In other words, if approved, they serve again. If not, they are gone.

General Solution 2: throw the bums out

I keep coming back to this because it is the only option we fully control. Simply throw the bums out. Though this will take more time, the people should take an oath if the leaders will not that every current office holder at any level of government that chooses not to renew their oath of office, shall hereby be voted against and thus thrown out of office. No second chances. And we encourage some people from the non-political side of life to take their places. Once they are gone, we get a fresh start.

General Solution 3: initiative, referendum, and recall

The people need to add an amendment to the Constitution to provide the rights of initiative, referendum, and recall. Initiative as it exists in the states is the ability of citizens to suggest legislation for consideration by a state legislature. Referendum is the passage or rejection of a proposed law by the citizens of a state in a statewide vote. Recall is the ability to recall a candidate once he or she has been elected if he/she is not fulfilling the promised duties of office.

The most important of these at this time is the right of initiative, though the others are also necessary. There is no such thing provided for in our Constitution for federal leaders. Here's why.

You may recall the civics lessons along the way in which we discussed the U.S. as a constitutional democracy. In such a democracy we have a Constitution and representative government. Initiative is a structure of a direct democracy in which the people make the laws without representatives. In order to offer countervailing power to the people against the powerful coalition of the President, Congress, unions, corporations, and to an extent, even the Supreme Court, the people need the power to submit legislation for consideration.

The other good part of this is that it would help more people to be more active their government. Therefore, it would be tough for the scoundrels to continually snooker We the people as they have been doing for too long.

An amendment to the Constitution (Citizens' Initiatives Constitutional Amendment) is already in process at http://www.cusdi.org/. This can be the first step of the process and then would come the formation of the committees funded under the power of the Amendment by the government. This in process amendment is good to hop-on and support.

beg you, if you have read this far in this book, to please go to http://www.cusdi.org/ and read their proposal on Initiative.

The folks at the web site address shown above have put together a Citizens "Athenian" Initiatives Amendment which focuses on the Initiative part of this recommendation. It is excellent. This is the first of the process.

Encourage your congressman to get the amendment passed to start Americans on a path to better assure that we are protected from electing corrupt do-fusses and buffoons in the future. Additionally, get your state representatives and state senators involved to begin the amendment process in your state.

This is the closest thing I have seen since I first saw the classic movie, Meet John Doe starring Gary Cooper with Barbara Stanwyck, Edward Arnold, Walter Brennan, Spring Byington.

The unscrupulous politician is portrayed by Edward Arnold in this movie but in your districts and my district they have different names. But they are actors nonetheless. Picture Gary Cooper as John Doe rallying all of us other John Doe's to work on the Citizens' Initiatives' Constitutional Amendment campaign. And then they all lived happily ever after. It would be nice.

By the way, the framers of the Constitutional Democracy of the United States were smart very men. They were not, however aware of the Athenian democracy notions as archaeology had yet to discover the materials. In fact, it was not for over 100 years after the founding fathers put together our government that this other information became available. This would have been a great-add-on to the Constitution, had the founding fathers known about it. Through the amendment process, we can make it part of the Constitution.

A reading of the U.S. Constitution is always a refreshing wake-up experience. The Constitution was not written for slithering rogues or despicable thieves. It was written for good God-fearing people. This amendment and the Initiatives and other amendments that may follow are needed because our politicians have lost their fear of God and their fear of shame and worse than that, their fear of the people.

The corporate god of greed and the self-god of pomposity and self-importance, and the lure of the comfortable life of an elite have misdirected many of our representatives to be substantially less than they can be. So, the people have no choice but to take back the government using both the same constitutional instrument that has guided us so far, as well as the notions discussed in this section. Let us hope and pray that our representatives are merely good men and women gone bad, rather than bad men and women. The words of our Second President, John Adams, are haunting as they appear to be written for our times:

- "We have no government armed with power capable of contending with human passions unbridled by morality and religion... Our constitution was made only for a moral and religious people. It is wholly inadequate to the government of any other."

- "The church is the moral compass of society."

- "We have no constitution which functions in the absence of a moral people."

- "A standing army, however necessary it may be at some times, is always dangerous to the Liberties of the People."

The words of John Quincy Adams, our sixth president give what one would think might be reason for his election. Though he had big issues before and during his presidency, and he never was popular, he had a message well worth hearing: Perhaps these words are even more haunting than those of his Father, John Adams, the second President.

"Men, in a word, must necessarily be controlled either by a power within them or by a power without them; either by the word of God or by the strong arm of man: either by the Bible or by the bayonet."

"The highest glory of the American Revolution was this: It connected in one indissoluble bond the principles of civil government with the principles of Christianity.

"The experience of all former ages had shown that of all human governments, democracy was the most unstable, fluctuating and short-lived."

Ironically for a man with such insights, Quincy Adams was chosen for the presidency in 1821, not by the people but by the House of Representatives. He and the other two candidates had lost both the popular vote and the electoral vote. Andrew Jackson was the high vote getter but even he did not have the majority. Quincy Adams won the election since the 12th amendment of the constitution prescribes that when no candidate has a majority of electoral votes, the election will be decided among the top three by the House of Representatives. Quincy Adams was an unpopular president and failed to win a second term... but these quotes live on.

One more point: Under the original provisions of the Constitution, the only direct election of any Federal representative was to the House of Representatives. The Presidential system was indirect via the Electoral College and Senators were selected by a state's legislature. Under the provisions of the 17th amendment to the Constitution, Senate elections became direct elections within each individual state.

This change had to have been done via an amendment because it was directly changing what was originally stated in the Constitution. The current version of the Citizens' Initiatives Constitutional Amendment is already well framed but requires several more edits to be in final form. Then, just as the 12th (President) and 17th (Senate) amendments changed how the voice of the people is expressed, so also will the 28th (People) amendment. Let us work so that we can celebrate.

General Solution 4: use the courts.

Find a good trial lawyer. Give them half and take action against the corporations and those who tacitly break our laws. Trial Lawyers may have a moral compass that always points to their wallets; but they cannot win without being very adept at the law. There are many abuses of the people's rights today and when Congress chooses to take no action, We the People, collectively or individually can find ourselves a good lawyer and use our right to redress.

Until all the judges are owned by corporations and hopefully that will never happen, this may prove to be a very effective way to curb abuse of all kinds. We do need to learn how to sue our legislators for lack of representation. Find a good lawyer and let's take that one on. If your employer fires you and hires someone with an H-1B visa or an illegal, for example, sue them.

The courts are a last resort for the American way. Let's use the courts. Let's find some lawyers who are willing to do this work pro bono, and let's make them famous. The courts can help us gain justice by Civil Law to overcome the criminals, often our legislators, in our midst.

General Solution 5: pay attention

I have a great and wonderful friend who like me is Catholic. We don't evaluate the extent of each other's' Catholicism but we respect each other's word as being the truth. Francis X. Kurilla was an IBM Administrative Executive in the New Jersey Area. While he was approaching retirement age, he unexpectedly passed on to the Lord. He was a great friend. Frank told me a long time ago about a real situation that occurred in his church.

The Church was Catholic but there were a lot of European customs exercised during the mass that occurred in his church. At Easter Midnight Mass, his priest would go off on a multi-hour sermon or so it was relayed by Frank.

During the sermon, the priest would look around and see a few "nodding" parishioners. While in the midst of a very serious sermon or readings, both being chanted, the priest, without missing a note, would chant, "Be attentive!" These admonitions were so well blended that if you were not paying attention, you would be startled and if you were paying attention, you would almost not notice. The moral of the story of course is, "Pay Attention!"

Please note that solutions 1 to 4 have some prospects for success only if we want them to be successful. Remember "nothing in life, worth having, is easy." That goes for the right to life, liberty, and the pursuit of happiness. While you work on the real solutions, *pay attention* to your government. Get to know your representatives at all levels. Remember who works for whom.

Send them emails and faxes and real mail and occasionally a registered letter just to get on their true fan list. Prod your local radio and TV personalities. Hound legislators about the major issues of the constituency and ask them to have a program in English each week that talks about the legislation they are working on, what passed last week, and who voted for what and what does it mean. Include yourself in their lives.

This is the ultimate reality show in an age of no writers. Talking about a reality show. How much better can you get? If you can coax the Ozzie family and the Hulk and his family to show up at a legislative session, you can actually see the same stuff on three different TV shows. That's Reality TV.

Our legislators have failed us so miserably that they deserve nothing less than public shame. Unfortunately, since Hollywood threw shame out the window over thirty years ago, there is no longer such a thing. But, if there were, our legislators would suffer from it. Maybe we can bring some shame back when we let our legislators go. That way the new guys would have to be concerned about it.

At Marywood University, for years, until I was fired for running for Public Office, I had the pleasure of teaching Operational Management. That's the part of the business in which more than 95% of the people work. When I taught my students about quality, I always told them the first message of quality is to pay attention. Pay attention to quality and with no additional programs, quality will get better. That's the message in General Solution 5. Pay attention.

Among all the other things that workers are thinking about when they come to work, they are thinking about making the product better or doing a better job or being more pleasant if they have a service mission. But, they are also thinking of the Super-bowl, the Yankees, their girlfriends, etc. in other words, if they can be paying attention to the mission at hand, that will bring its own set of quality rewards to the matter at hand. So, "pay attention" to what your government is doing; and you can help bring about a higher quality government. It can happen. Yes it can!

These five General Solutions are just the start but, they are a very good start to getting this country back on the right track

Other books by Brian Kelly: (amazon.com, and Kindle)

Taxation W/O Representation How to solve the problem of poor representation before all the Tea is gone!
Delete the EPA Third Edition You won't believe how nasty the EPA really is!
Wipe Out All Student Debt Now! How to improve the economy with one bold move
Boost Social Security Now! Hey Buddy Can You Spare a Dime?
The Birth of American Football. From the first college game in 1869 to the last Super Bowl
Obamacare: A One-Line Repeal Congress must get this done.
A Wilkes-Barre Christmas Story A wonderful town makes Christmas all the better
A Boy, A Bike, A Train, and a Christmas Miracle A Christmas story that will melt your heart
Pay-to-Go America-First Immigration Fix
Legalizing Illegal Aliens Via Resident Visas Americans-first plan saves $Trillions. Learn how!
60 Million Illegal Aliens in America!!! A simple, America-first solution.
The Bill of Rights By Founder James Madison Refresh *your knowledge of the specific rights for all*
Great Players in Army Football Great Army Football played by great players..
Great Coaches in Army Football Army's coaches are all great.
Great Moments in Army Football Army Football at its best.
Great Moments in Florida Gators Football Gators Football from the start. This is the book.
Great Moments in Clemson Football CU Football at its best. This is the book.
Great Moments in Florida Gators Football Gators Football from the start. This is the book.
The **Constitution Companion.** A Guide to Reading and Comprehending the Constitution
The Constitution by Hamilton, Jefferson, & Madison – Big type and in English
PATERNO: The Dark Days After Win # 409. Sky began to fall within days of win # 409.
JoePa 409 Victories: Say No More! Winningest Division I-A football coach ever
American College Football: The Beginning From before day one football was played.
Great Coaches in Alabama Football Challenging the coaches of every other program!
Great Coaches in Penn State Football the Best Coaches in PSU's football program
Great Players in Penn State Football The best players in PSU's football program
Great Players in Notre Dame Football The best players in ND's football program
Great Coaches in Notre Dame Football The best coaches in any football program
Great Players in Alabama Football from Quarterbacks to offensive Linemen Greats!
Great Moments in Alabama Football AU Football from the start. This is the book.
Great Moments in Penn State Football PSU Football, start--games, coaches, players,
Great Moments in Notre Dame Football ND Football, start, games, coaches, players
Cross Country With the Parents A great trip from East Coast to West with the kids
Seniors, Social Security & the Minimum Wage. Things seniors need to know.
How to Write Your First Book and Publish It with CreateSpace
The US Immigration Fix--It's all in here. Finally, an answer.
I had a Dream IBM Could be #1 Again The title is self-explanatory
WineDiets.Com Presents The Wine Diet Learn how to lose weight while having fun.
Wilkes-Barre, PA; Return to Glory Wilkes-Barre City's return to glory
Geoffrey Parsons' Epoch... The Land of Fair Play Better than the original.
The Bill of Rights 4 Dummmies! This is the best book to learn about your rights.
Sol Bloom's Epoch ...Story of the Constitution The best book to learn the Constitution
America 4 Dummmies! All Americans should read to learn about this great country.
The Electoral College 4 Dummmies! How does it really work?
The All-Everything Machine Story about IBM's finest computer server.
ThankYou IBM! This book explains how IBM was beaten in the computer marketplace by neophytes

Brian has written 144 books in total. Other books can be found at amazon.com/author/brianwkelly

www.ingramcontent.com/pod-product-compliance
Lightning Source LLC
Chambersburg PA
CBHW071708090426
42738CB00009B/1712